A Prayer Book
for Today's Catholic

Dedication

**To God the Father
in whose family we all share.**

A Prayer Book
for Today's Catholic

Monsignor Michael J. Buckley

CHARIS
SERVANT PUBLICATIONS
ANN ARBOR, MICHIGAN

Charis Books is an imprint of Servant Publications especially designed
to serve Roman Catholics.

Published by Servant Publications
P.O. Box 8617
Ann Arbor, Michigan 48107

00 01 02 03   10 9 8 7 6 5 4 3 2 1

Printed in the United States of America
ISBN 1-56955-183-9

LIBRARY OF CONGRESS CATALOGING-IN-PUBLICATION DATA

Buckley, Michael J.
A prayer book for today's Catholic / Michael J. Buckley.
    p.   cm.
ISBN 1-56955-183-9 (alk. paper)
1. Catholic Church—Prayer-books and devotions—English.
I. Title.
BX2110.B846 20000
242'.802—dc21   99-086139

Contents

Part 3: Special Prayers for People,
Occasions, and Needs

Part 1

Prayers for the Seasons

The Season of Advent
A Season of Waiting and Expectancy

The church is the "bride" of Christ waiting for the second coming of her "Bridegroom." We know that this will happen in God's good time, as God is always faithful to his promises. He proved this fidelity when, according to his messianic promise, he sent his only Son, born as a child in Bethlehem. Christmas is our assurance that Christ will come to us again at the end of the world, not as a baby in a stable but as the King of glory seated on his throne.

Ever since Jesus' ascension into heaven, Christians have awaited the second coming of Christ when he will be revealed to us in all his glory. This aspect of *waiting* conveys the real spiritual meaning of Advent. We live in the in-between period of the history of salvation. Christ has already come to Bethlehem as a baby to show us how much his Father loves us. This is the *first coming*.

We who have received him in faith wait in joyful hope for his *second coming* at the end of the world. We do not know when this will happen. So during the season of Advent we watch and wait in hope. In the meantime, like John the Baptist, who prepared for Christ's first coming, we too are called to "prepare the way" for his second coming.

There is great *expectancy* and joy in the four weeks leading up to Christmas. The prayers and readings at

Mass during Advent are full of hope, reminding us that the darkness of night will soon be dispelled by the brightness of the coming of the Lord. Isaiah 9:1 says it all: "The people that walked in darkness have seen a great light" (NJB).

Like the dark days of winter that will give way to the brightness and promise of spring, so the light of Christ's second coming will give meaning to all of this life's hardships and sufferings. When Christ comes again, his presence will exceed all our dreams: "What no eye has seen and no ear has heard, what the mind of man cannot visualise; all that God has prepared for those who love him" (1 Cor 2:9 NJB). This is the joy and promise of Advent.

* * * *

The Advent mystery is the beginning of the end of all in us that is not yet Christ.

Thomas Merton

This then is to watch: to be detached from what is present, and to live in what is unseen; to live in the thought of Christ as he came once, and as he will come again; to desire his second coming, from our affectionate and grateful remembrance of his first.

John Henry Newman

Return, O God of love, return,
Earth is a tiresome place;
How long shall we thy children mourn
Our absence from thy face?

Early American Hymn

O quickly come, great King of all;
Reign all around us, and within;
Let sin no more our souls enthrall,
Let pain and sorrow die with sin;
O quickly come: for you alone
Can make your scattered people one.

O quickly come, true Life of all;
For death is mighty all around;
On every home his shadows fall,
On every heart his mark is found:
O quickly come: for grief and pain
Can never cloud your glorious reign.

O quickly come, sure Light of all,
For gloomy night broods o'er our way;
And fainting souls begin to fall
With every weary watching for the day:
O quickly come: for round your throne
No eye is blind, no night is known.

L. Tuttiett

O come, O come, Emmanuel,
And ransom captive Israel;
That mourns in lonely exile here,
Until the Son of God appear.

O come, thou Rod of Jesse, free
Thine own from Satan's tyranny;
From depths of hell thy people save,
And give them victory o'er the grave.

O come, thou Day-Spring, come and cheer
Our spirits by thine Advent here;
Disperse the gloomy clouds of night,
And death's dark shadows put to flight.
Rejoice! Rejoice! Emmanuel
Shall come to thee, O Israel.

Latin, ninth century,
trans. by John M. Neale

Exert, O Lord, your power and come: that by your protection we may be freed from the imminent dangers of our sins and be saved by your mercy.
Exert, O Lord, your power and come: that they who trust in your goodness may speedily be delivered from all adversity.

Roman Missal, *1843*

Stir up, O Lord, our hearts to prepare the ways of your only begotten Son: that by his coming we may be enabled to serve you with pure minds.

Roman Missal, *1843*

Make haste, O Lord, and delay not, but grant us the assistance of your heavenly grace: that they who trust in your goodness may be relieved by the comfort of your coming.

Roman Missal, *1843*

Preparation for the Second Coming

Father, we praise you that from the very beginning you gave your people hope for the future by promising them that you would send a Messiah who would be their Savior, Leader, and King. This promise so sustained your people in their troubled times in exile and persecution that they never ceased to believe that you were their God and they were your people.

You were always true to your promises and to the covenant you made with them. They had to wait patiently in hope until the fullness of time, when the Messiah came as one of them. Your gift of your own Son was the crowning glory of their faith and hope and gave meaning to the centuries of their waiting.

We believe that in good times and bad you have always watched over us with gentleness and compassion. Teach us, Father, to wait with patience and unshakable faith until the day when your Son Jesus

Christ comes again in all his glory to take us and the whole of creation home to you.

In this season of Advent, as we celebrate the first coming of your Son to us in Bethlehem, may we joyfully anticipate the day when Christ will come again.

May our Advent season be a preparation for the day when we are taken into the joy of heaven, where waiting will be no more and all our hopes will be fulfilled.

M.B.

Spirit of Gratitude

Lord Jesus, your coming among us to share our human condition has transformed our lives. You have made us a people of hope and joy, because we know that you will always be with us, encouraging and supporting us in every situation. We will never be alone again, and this is why we want to prepare ourselves in our minds and hearts, so that we will celebrate your birthday in a spirit of gratitude for all you have done and are doing for us.

Send your Holy Spirit to us, so that we spend these weeks of preparation thinking about what your coming among us truly means and about the mystery of your love for us, which surpasses all our hopes and expectations.

M.B.

Spiritual Renewal

Holy Spirit, help us prepare for the great feast of Christmas. This will mean a spiritual renewal of our lives, so that when Christ comes he will find that the path to our minds and hearts has been made straight and cleared of obstacles. Give us the wisdom to appreciate the true value of Advent, and change the pattern of our lives, so that this Christmas Christ will find us more ready to receive him in gladness and joy. Breathe into us a spirit of thanksgiving that the long hours of waiting are nearly over; that Christ our Lord stands at the door waiting for us to welcome him into our homes. Give us the vision to walk into the light of Christian faith and hope, remembering that he who comes and whose birthday we celebrate is the Light of our world, dispelling the darkness and giving meaning to our lives. May every day of the rest of our lives be a preparation for the second advent when Christ will come again in all his glory to us.

M.B.

The Season of Christmas
A Season of Celebration

In this season we celebrate the birth of Jesus our Savior; the work of our redemption has already begun. He is Emmanuel—God with us—and in him we find new life. His final coming at the end of the world may still be far off, but his coming at Bethlehem has changed the course of human history. The world will never be the same again.

During the Christmas season, we celebrate two great feasts, Christmas and Epiphany. As in Advent, the season has a double significance, commemorating the coming of Jesus in human flesh and his second coming. We rejoice in the Lord's coming at Bethlehem which gives us the assurance and hope that he will come again in glory. The wonder and thanksgiving felt at Christmas is but a foretaste of our future gladness, when Christ our Savior will finally be revealed as Lord of the universe.

Pagans kept solstice festivals to celebrate the return of light. With joy and hope they looked forward to spring. How much more joyful and hopeful are we now that the light and life of Christ have dawned.

* * * *

Now to the Lord sing praises,
All you within this place,
And with true love and brotherhood
Each other now embrace;
This holy tide of Christmas
Doth bring redeeming grace.
O tidings of comfort and joy,
Comfort and joy;
O tidings of comfort and joy!

Traditional Carol

Lord, you have come to us as a small child, but you have brought us the greatest of all gifts, the gift of eternal love. Caress us with your tiny hands, embrace us with your tiny arms, and pierce our hearts with your soft, sweet cries.

Saint Bernard of Clairvaux

Father, you make us young again at Christmas when we thrill to the wonder of the birth of your Son. The magic of love in the air lifts us up and warms us in the cold bleakness of winter. It is a time to make us hope again. You are never far away from us in our needs, and you will not be outdone in generosity, as you sent us your Son as a baby to be one of our family. Help me, Lord, this Christmas to think of life, love, and happiness as I share in the celebration of the birth of Jesus your Son with those whom you have given me as my family.

M.B.

Christmas Day
December 25

Today a Savior is born for us. In the stillness of the night, God enters human history through the birth of his Son Jesus, our peace and hope. In him we praise God our good Father for giving us so great a gift. Like the shepherds, in the stable of Bethlehem we discover in this baby the measure of God's compassionate love for us. Through the birth of Jesus, we are reborn.

* * * *

O God, who has enlightened this most sacred night by the brightness of him who is the true Light; grant that we who have known the mysteries of this Light on earth may likewise come to the enjoyment of it in heaven.

Roman Missal, *1834*

Almighty God, who has poured upon us the new light of your incarnate Word; grant that the same light enkindled in our hearts may shine forth in our lives; through Jesus Christ our Lord.

Sarum Rite, Christmas Mass at Dawn

Make me pure, Lord: thou art holy;
Make me meek, Lord: thou were lowly;
Now beginning, and always:
Now begin, on Christmas Day.

Gerard Manley Hopkins, S.J.

O holy Child of Bethlehem!
Descend to us, we pray;
Cast out our sin, and enter in,
Be born in us today.
We hear the Christmas angels
The great glad tidings tell;
O come to us, abide with us,
Our Lord Emmanuel!

Phillips Brooks

Yea, Lord, we greet thee,
Born this happy morning,
Jesus, to thee be all glory given;
Word of the Father,
Now in flesh appearing.
O come, let us adore him,
Christ the Lord!

John Francis Wade

Loving Father, help us to remember the birth of Jesus, that we may share in the song of the angels, the gladness of the shepherds, and the wisdom of the wise men. Close the door of hate and open the door of love all over the world. Let kindness come with every gift and good desires with every greeting. Deliver us from evil by the blessing which Christ brings and teach us to be merry with clean hearts. May the Christmas morning make us happy to be your children, and the Christmas evening bring us to our beds with grateful thoughts, forgiving and forgiven for Jesus' sake.

Robert Louis Stevenson

Christ is born, give glory. Christ comes from heaven, meet him. Christ is on earth, be exalted. All the earth sing unto the Lord, and sing praises in gladness, all you people, for he has been glorified.

Eastern Orthodox Church

Sweet Child of Bethlehem, grant that we may share with all our hearts this profound mystery of Christmas. Put into the hearts of everyone this peace for which they sometimes seek so desperately, and which you alone can give them. Help them to know one another better and to live as brothers and sisters of the same Father.

Pope John XXIII

May Joy Shine Through Me Today

Lord Jesus, you brought joy into this world and into so many lives. You shared your joy with shepherds at your birth, with the guests at the wedding feast in Cana, with the children who clung to you, the lepers who cried out to you, with the people who crowded around you to listen to your message of hope, with Mary your mother whom you loved more than anyone and with whom you shared your life. We thank you that this joy was not destroyed by your death but came renewed into our world by your resurrection. May the light of your joy shine through me today so that I may reflect it to those around me and lift them up in hope and joy.

M.B.

The Holy Family of Jesus, Mary, and Joseph
Sunday After Christmas Day

God sets before us the Holy Family of Nazareth as the model for all families. The family unit is the basic structure on which human society is built. A good Christian family is a powerful witness to our world of God's love revealed for us in the example of Jesus and his relationship to his mother, Mary, and Joseph.

* * * *

For All Families
Lord Jesus, you blessed the human family by spending most of your life with your mother and Joseph at home in Nazareth. There you grew up, and, by your obedient loving presence, you raised the dignity of the family to a pinnacle.

Today we pray for all families, especially those in which there is discord between children and step-parents. May children and parents be open and kind and respectful to each other. May their homes be blessed with your presence, so that families may grow together in love and peace and a true appreciation of one another.

M.B.

For Those Suffering Pain in Marriage

Jesus, Lover of the family, I pray for your blessing on all those who suffer the pain of rejection in marriage. Many feel so emotionally deserted by their spouse that they feel worthless. They are unable to share many hurtful memories with anyone, so the secrets lie buried within them. May those memories never fester into a bitterness that destroys. As they pick up the pieces of their lives, be with them, Lord, and gently lead them to a restored sense of self-value; give them the courage to face the future with calm hope and peace. Heal them, Lord, as only you know how.

M.B.

For Parents Who Search for Children

Lord Jesus, your mother Mary sought for you for three days when she lost you in Jerusalem. You caused her anxiety, wondering where you were. Yes, you were about your Father's business; even so, it is strange that one so sensitive and caring as you caused so much anguish to Mary and Joseph. I pray for all parents who search for their children, flesh of their own flesh, and want to know how they are faring. Many parents grieve at the loss of children who no longer contact them, who cause them undue anxiety and pain. Jesus, I pray that parents trust their children to your tender care. Good Shepherd that you are, may you bring back to the fold of the family the lambs that have strayed.

M.B.

Teach Us That Love Never Ends

Lord Jesus, as you witnessed to the beauty of human love at the wedding feast in Cana, you gave us a better understanding of married love in this life and in the world to come. There's a power manifested in Christian marriage: A couple's love for each other is an expression of our love for you—the Bridegroom of the church.

Teach us that love never ends. I have seen the lonely tears of grieving widows and widowers. But their faith in you as their resurrection was stronger than their grief. Finding consolation in your promise of eternal life, they no longer grieved as those who have no hope. In heaven, Lord, all love shall be made complete; the companionship experienced in this life will grow to fulfillment. When we are with you and each other in heaven, there will be no more tears or parting; love and life will be forever. Thank you, Lord, for this family comfort.

M.B.

The Epiphany of the Lord
January 6

This feast celebrates the revealing (epiphany) of the Messiah to the Gentiles. This is symbolized by wise men from the East coming to Bethlehem. Guided by a star, they came to worship the infant King, bringing him gifts of gold, frankincense, and myrrh. In the story of these Gentile worshipers, we see God's Son being revealed to the whole world.

* * * *

The star, a sign of the Lord's birth, has appeared in the sky to invite us to detach ourselves from the love of earthly things and raise ourselves heavenward that we may understand that through Christ's birth we shall be flooded with new light.

Aelred of Rievaulx

Hail, O Sun, O blessed Light,
Sent into the world by night!
Let thy rays and heavenly powers
Shine in these dark souls of ours;
For most duly
Thou art truly
God and man, we do confess:
Hail, O Sun of Righteousness!

W. Austin

Grant us grace to see thee, Lord,
Present in thy holy Word;
May we imitate thee now,
And be pure, as pure art thou;
That we like to thee may be
At thy great Epiphany;
And may praise thee, ever blest,
God in man made manifest.

Charles Wordsworth

O God, who by the direction of a star did this day manifest your only Son to the Gentiles, mercifully grant that we, who now know you by faith, may come at length to see the glory of your majesty.

Roman Missal, *1843*

Mercifully look down, O Lord, on the offerings of your church. Though gold, frankincense, and myrrh are no longer offered, what was signified by those offerings is sacrificed and received in the Mass: Jesus Christ, your Son our Lord.

Roman Missal, *1843*

Guide Us by the Light of the Holy Spirit

Heavenly Father, who by the light of a star led the wise men to the city of David where they worshiped your Son, guide us by the light of your Holy Spirit into the presence of the same Jesus to worship him and to offer him the gift of the loving service of our lives.

M.B.

Lord, help us to follow the Light of Christ by faith, even when its brightness and presence is hidden from our eyes.

M.B.

Jesus Is God the Father's Gift to Us

God the Father, we praise and thank you that you sent your Son Jesus to heal and reconcile the world. No one is excluded from your love and forgiveness, because you are the Father of all. Kings and shepherds, rich and poor find their home in the stable at Bethlehem. We offer our gift of love to the infant Jesus whose humanity reaches out to everyone, providing a purpose and fulfillment in life. Just as the star guided the wise men, so the Holy Spirit leads us to find your Son who is the Light of the world. May he light up our minds and hearts, so that we may be filled with peace and joy on this special day when you revealed your Son to the whole world.

M.B.

Jesus, Lover of the Human Race

Jesus, Savior of the world, you are the Center of your Father's plan for our salvation. In you we find a sign of the Father's love for us. We thank you that you loved being human and shared completely in our life, except for sin. Help us to love who we are, as we strive to become who you would have us be. Like you, may we grow in our awareness and knowledge of God the Father's love for us.

M.B.

The Holy Spirit as Our Guide

Holy Spirit of God, you were in the star that led the wise men across the desert. Be in our lives so that, like them, in our pilgrimage we may follow Christ our Star and never lose sight of him because of worldly distractions. We too can become an epiphany—a revealing—of God to others if we remain faithful to our Christian calling.

M.B.

Mary, Encourage Us to Share

Mary, Mother of the infant Jesus, you shared your Son with everyone near and far. You realized and showed us, by your example, that Jesus was for all seasons and all peoples. Encourage us to be generous in sharing our Christian gifts with others so that they too may come and find with you a meaning and purpose for their lives.

M.B.

Joseph, Encourage Us to Protect the Gift

Joseph, protector of Mary and her infant Jesus, be near us and by your example encourage us to protect the very precious gift of faith that has been given to us by the Holy Spirit. Help us to be gentle but firm whenever our belief in Jesus' divinity is questioned, and let the light of our faith shine out in all that we say and do.

M.B.

The Baptism of the Lord
Sunday After January 6

The Holy Spirit came down upon Jesus at his baptism in the Jordan River, and a voice assured John the Baptist and witnessed to others that Jesus was the Father's beloved Son. The Holy Spirit comes down on each one of us and helps us to live our Christian lives so that we are faithful to our baptism.

* * * *

O Father, bless the children
Brought here to your gate;
Lift up their fallen nature,
Restore their lost estate;
Renew your image in them,
And own them, by this sign,

Your very sons and daughters,
Newborn of birth divine.

O Jesus, Lord, receive them;
Your loving arms of old
Were opened wide to welcome
The children to your fold:
Let these, baptized, and dying,
Then rising from the dead,
Henceforth be living members
Of thee, their living head.

O Holy Spirit, keep them;
Dwell with them to the last,
Till all the fight is ended
And all the storms are past.
Renew the gift baptismal,
From strength to strength, till each,
The troublesome waves o'ercoming,
The land of life shall reach.

John Ellerton

Pour Out Your Blessings

By God's gift, through water and the Holy Spirit, we
are reborn to everlasting life. Lord, in your goodness,
may you continue to pour out your blessings upon all
your sons and daughters. May you make them always,
wherever they may be, faithful members of his holy
people and send your peace upon all.

M.B.

The Presence of the Holy Spirit

Holy Spirit, we praise you that you come to all those who are cleansed through the healing waters of baptism. Through your presence, new life is given to each baptized person. By baptism they share in the risen life of the Lord Jesus. They become members of Christ's family, his church. We are reborn through your Spirit, and for this unique grace we praise and thank you. Just as the passage through water signifies our journey from the death of sin to the life of grace, so through your grace we are enabled to live the new life promised by our Lord. We pray today for all Christians everywhere that they may be true to their special calling.

M.B

Parents and Sponsors

We pray today for our parents and godparents and thank them for the support they have given us, encouraging us to live the Christian life. We pray that you will bless them for their Christian faith and steadfastness, which has been a constant witness to us. May we in our turn live true to the gospel message of Jesus Christ our Lord and Savior, in whose name we make this prayer.

M.B.

The Season of Lent
A Season of Self-Examination and Sacrifice

Lent is a time for us to face ourselves and our lifestyle. We cannot keep on foolishly indulging ourselves, and so this season we make sacrifices in our style of daily living. We realize, perhaps gradually at first, that the only way to grow spiritually is through the cross. It is held before our eyes in all the readings at Mass to remind us of the price Jesus paid for our salvation.

We *renounce* our selfishness in terms of material possessions to *announce* the power of Christ's resurrection. Every renunciation is for annunciation, just as our death to self is an ongoing process into the life of the risen Christ. The seven weeks of renunciation prepare us to be ready and more aware of the significance of the resurrection. The gospel message of Lent is clear: If we die with him, we shall rise with him.

Lent puts before us the whole mystery of salvation through which God the Father's merciful love for us has been revealed in the passion, death, and resurrection of his Son.

* * * *

God, being rich in faithful love, through the great love with which he loved us, even when we were dead in our sins, brought us to life with Christ ... and raised us up with him and gave us a place with him in heaven, in Christ Jesus.

This was to show for all ages to come, through his goodness towards us in Christ Jesus, how extraordinarily rich he is in grace. Because it is by grace that you have been saved, through faith; not by anything of your own, but by a gift from God; not by anything that you have done, so that nobody can claim the credit. We are God's work of art, created in Christ Jesus for the good works which God has already designated to make up our way of life.

EPHESIANS 2:4-10 NJB

Lord, who throughout these forty days,
For us did fast and pray,
Teach us with thee to mourn our sins,
And close by thee to stay.

As you with Satan did contend,
And did the victory win,
O give us strength in thee to fight
In thee to conquer sin.

As thou did bear hunger and thirst,
So teach us, gracious Lord,
To die to self, and chiefly live
By thy most holy Word.

And through these days of penitence,
And through thy Passion-tide,
Yea, evermore, in life and death,
Jesus with us abide.

Abide with us, that so, this life
Of suffering overpast,
An Easter of unending joy
We may attain at last.

Charles Hernaman

Wilt thou forgive that sin, where I begun,
Which is my sin, though it were done before?
Wilt thou forgive those sins through which I run,
And do run still, though still I do deplore?
When thou hast done, thou hast not done,
For I have more.

Wilt thou forgive that sin, by which I won
Others to sin, and made my sin their door?
Wilt thou forgive that sin which I did shun
A year or two, but wallowed in a score?
When thou hast done, thou hast not done,
For I have more.

I have a sin of fear that when I've spun
My last thread, I shall perish on the shore;
Swear by thyself, that at my death thy Son
Shall shine as he shines now, and heretofore.
And having done that, thou hast done,
I fear no more.

John Donne

The trees around me flourish and spread their branches. But I am hemmed in by the guilt that surrounds me, and I wither because of the poison of sin within me. Ah Lord, you are the only remedy. I accept that while I remain on earth I must endure hardship, and must be spiritually destitute. I may enjoy the affection of friends, and the hospitality of strangers, but these are only brief flashes of light in the darkness. Let my suffering bring me true contrition, that I may receive your forgiveness, and so be made fit for the everlasting joy of heaven.

The Exeter Book, tenth century

Renewal of Faith, Hope, and Love

Lord Jesus, give me the courage of faith, so that I may always confess my allegiance to you especially when times are difficult and suffering seems to take over my life. Even in the middle of your passion, when you entrusted your life to the Father, you taught me to hope and trust in the fatherhood of God however straitened I might be in trials and tribulations.

Hope was the secret of your calling and magnetism, and I pray that I may be drawn this Lent to know and love you as I have previously, before the world with its false sense of values lured me away from you. Renew my faith, hope, and love, so that at the end of this season I may be more the person you would have me be.

M.B.

Draw Me to God and to Silence

Holy Spirit of God, I pray that you will touch me this Lent and turn my life toward you in such a way that I desire nothing other than to do the will of my loving Father. Warm my cold heart and set me on fire with love for you, so that all my selfish thoughts will be burned away, and encourage me to turn to you with undivided openness and a spirit of silence.

Spirit of God, teach me to be silent, that I may hear your gentle whisper telling me how much my Father loves me. May I use this special season of grace and renewal to seek you more diligently. And when I have found you, may I never let you go.

M.B.

Mary, May I Stand With You

Mary, my Mother, I thank you for your great love for your Son Jesus. You never failed him throughout his life, and at the end you stood by the foot of the cross. Be with me this Lent, so that in bad times as well as good I may stand with you as a sign of my love for your Son and my God, until the darkness of suffering and death give way to the unquenchable light of the resurrection.

M.B.

The Value of Self-Denial

Lord Jesus, even though you are always God, you humbled yourself and came among us in human form as our Servant and Friend. Give me an awareness of your unique sacrifice on our behalf and teach me to be humble in acknowledging that all my gifts come from you for the service of people and the spread of your kingdom. Teach me the value of self-denial, so that nothing of my vain self may manifest itself in anything that I say and do. May you live in me, so that in all my little acts of sacrifice the light of your resurrection may shine through and give them meaning.

M.B.

The Way of the Cross: A Biblical Form

From the earliest times, Christians have traced the footsteps of the Lord carrying his cross from Pilate's house to Golgotha, the crucifixion site. The Crusaders are said to have spread this devotion throughout Europe; for those unable to make the journey to Jerusalem, the "Way of the Cross" was set up in cathedrals and parish churches. To this day it is a worldwide feature of Christian devotion.

The number of "stations" of the cross has varied. At one time there were as many as thirty-six stations recalling the various highlights along the Via

Dolorosa (Sorrowful Road) of our Lord's last journey. In the sixteenth century, fourteen stations were chosen and approved by the Church; since the Second Vatican Council an additional station is often marked: the Resurrection of Jesus from the Dead. This is in keeping with the resurrection piety that permeates our whole approach to suffering and death.

* * * *

This response is said before each station:
We adore you, O Christ, and we bless you.
Because by your holy cross you have redeemed the
   world.

This prayer is said after each station:
I love you Jesus, my Love, above all things;
I repent with my whole heart for having offended
   you.
Never permit me to separate myself from you again.
Grant that I may love you always then do with me
   what you will.

First Station
Jesus Is Condemned to Death

Pilate came outside again and said to them, "Look, I am going to bring him out to you to let you see that I find no case." Jesus then came out wearing the crown of thorns and the purple robe. Pilate said, "Here is the man." When they saw him the chief priests and the guards shouted, "Crucify him! Crucify him!" Pilate said, "Take him yourselves and crucify him: I can find no case against him."

"We have a Law," the Jews replied "and according to that Law he ought to die, because he has claimed to be the Son of God."

When Pilate heard them say this his fears increased. Reentering the Praetorium, he said to Jesus, "Where do you come from?" But Jesus made no answer. Pilate then said to him, "Are you refusing to speak to me? Surely you know I have power to release you and I have power to crucify you?" "You would have no power over me" replied Jesus "if it had not been given you from above; that is why the one who handed me over to you has the greater guilt...."

So in the end Pilate handed him over to them to be crucified.

JOHN 19:4-11, 16

Second Station
Jesus Receives His Cross
Shoulder my yoke and learn from me, for I am gentle
and humble in heart, and you will find rest for your
souls. Yes, my yoke is easy and my burden light.

MATTHEW 11:29-30

Ours were the sufferings he bore,
ours the sorrows he carried.
But we, we thought of him as someone punished,
struck by God, and brought low.
Yet he was pierced through for our faults,
crushed for our sins.
On him lies a punishment that brings us peace,
and through his wounds we are healed.

ISAIAH 53:4-5

Third Station
Jesus Falls the First Time Under His Cross
We had all gone astray like sheep,
each taking his own way,
and Yahweh burdened him with the sins of all of us.
Harshly dealt with, he bore it humbly,
he never opened his mouth,
like a lamb that is led to the slaughter-house,
like a sheep that is dumb before its shearers
never opening its mouth.

By force and by law he was taken;
would anyone plead his cause?

ISAIAH 53:6-8

Yahweh my God, I call for help all day,
I weep to you all night;
may my prayer reach you
hear my cries for help;
for my soul is all troubled,
my life is on the brink of Sheol;
I am numbered among those who go down to the Pit,
a man bereft of strength.

PSALM 88:1-4

Fourth Station
Jesus Is Met by His Blessed Mother
When they failed to find him they went back to
Jerusalem looking for him everywhere.

Three days later, they found him in the Temple,
sitting among the doctors, listening to them, and ask-
ing them questions; and all those who heard him
were astounded at his intelligence and his replies.
They were overcome when they saw him, and his
mother said to him, "My child, why have you done
this to us? See how worried your father and I have
been, looking for you." "Why were you looking for
me?" he replied, "Did you not know that I must be
busy with my Father's affairs?"

LUKE 2:45-49

I sought him
whom my heart loves.
I sought but did not find him.

So I will rise and go through the City;
in the streets and the squares
I will seek him whom my heart loves.
...I sought but did not find him.

The watchmen came upon me
on their roads in the City:
"Have you seen him whom my heart loves?"
Scarcely had I passed them
than I found him whom my heart loves.

SONG OF SONGS 3:1-4

Fifth Station
The Cross Is Laid Upon Simon of Cyrene
They led him out to crucify him. They enlisted a passer-
by, Simon of Cyrene, father of Alexander and Rufus,
who was coming in from the country, to carry his
cross.

MARK 15:21

All I want is to know Christ and the power of his resurrection and to share his sufferings by reproducing
the pattern of his death. That is the way I can hope to
take my place in the resurrection of the dead. Not
that I have become perfect yet: I have not yet won,
but I am still running, trying to capture the prize for
which Christ Jesus captured me.

PHILIPPIANS 3:10-13

Sixth Station
Veronica Wipes the Face of Jesus
Without beauty, without majesty (we saw him),
no looks to attract our eyes;
a thing despised and rejected by men,
a man of sorrows and familiar with suffering,
a man to make people screen their faces;
he was despised and we took no account of him.

ISAIAH 53:2-3

As the crowds were appalled on seeing him
—so disfigured did he look
that he seemed no longer human—
so will the crowds be astonished at him,
and kings stand speechless before him;
for they shall see something never told
and witness something never heard before.

ISAIAH 52:14-15

My soul thirsts for God,
the God of life;
when shall I go to see
the face of God?

I have no food but tears,
day and night;
and all day long men say to me,
"Where is your God?"...
Why so downcast, my soul,

why do you sigh within me?
Put your hope in God: I shall praise him yet,
my saviour, my God.

PSALM 42:2-3, 5

Seventh Station
Jesus Falls the Second Time
His state was divine,
yet he did not cling
to his equality with God
but emptied himself
to assume the condition of a slave,
and became as men are;
and being as all men are,
he was humbler yet,
even to accepting death,
death on a cross.

PHILIPPIANS 2:6-8

During his life on earth, he offered up prayer and
entreaty, aloud and in silent tears, to the one who had
the power to save him out of death, and he submit-
ted so humbly that his prayer was heard. Although he
was Son, he learnt to obey through suffering; but
having been made perfect, he became for all who
obey him the source of eternal salvation and was
acclaimed by God with the title of high priest of the
order of Melchizedek.

HEBREWS 5:7-10

Eighth Station
The Women of Jerusalem Mourn for Our Lord
Large numbers of people followed him, and of women too, who mourned and lamented for him. But Jesus turned to them and said, "Daughters of Jerusalem, do not weep for me; weep rather for your-selves and for your children. For the days will surely come when people will say, 'Happy are those who are barren, the wombs that have never borne, the breasts that have never suckled!' Then they will begin to say to the mountains, 'Fall on us!'; to the hills, 'Cover us!' For if men use the green wood like this, what will happen when it is dry?"

LUKE 23:27-32

Ninth Station
Jesus Falls for the Third Time
I cannot understand my own behaviour. I fail to carry out the things I want to do, and I find myself doing the very things I hate.

ROMANS 7:15

The fact is, I know of nothing good living in me—living, that is, in my unspiritual self—for though the will to do what is good is in me, the performance is not, with the result that instead of doing the good things I want to do, I carry out the sinful things I do not want. When I act against my will, then it is not my true self doing it, but sin which lives in me.

In fact, this seems to be the rule, that every single time I want to do good it is something evil that comes to hand. In my inmost self I dearly love God's Law, but I can see that my body follows a different law that battles against the law which my reason dictates. This is what makes me a prisoner of that law of sin which lives inside my body.

What a wretched man I am! Who will rescue me from this body doomed to death?

ROMANS 7:18-24

You have given me an inch or two of life,
my life-span is nothing to you;
each man that stands on earth is only a puff of wind,
every man that walks, only a shadow,
and the wealth he amasses is only a puff of wind—
he does not know who will take it next.
So tell me, Lord, what can I expect?
My hope is in you.

PSALM 39:5-7

Yahweh, hear my prayer,
listen to my cry for help,
do not stay deaf to my crying.
I am your guest, and only for a time,
a nomad like all my ancestors.
Look away, let me draw breath,
before I go away and am no more!

PSALM 39:12-13

Tenth Station
Jesus Is Stripped of His Garments

When the soldiers had finished crucifying Jesus they took his clothing and divided it into four shares, one for each soldier. His undergarment was seamless, woven in one piece from neck to hem; so they said to one another, "Instead of tearing it, let's throw dice to decide who is to have it." In this way the words of scripture were fulfilled:

They shared out my clothing among them.
They cast lots for my clothes.
This is exactly what the soldiers did.

JOHN 19:23-24

While they were there the time came for her to have her child, and she gave birth to a son, her first-born. She wrapped him in swaddling clothes, and laid him in a manger because there was no room for them at the inn.

LUKE 2:6-7

You are God's chosen race, his saints; he loves you, and you should be clothed in sincere compassion, in kindness and humility, gentleness and patience. Bear with one another; forgive each other as soon as a quarrel begins. The Lord has forgiven you; now you must do the same. Over all these clothes, to keep them together and complete them, put on love. And may the peace of Christ reign in your hearts, because it is for this that you were called together as parts of one body. Always be thankful.

COLOSSIANS 3:12-15

Eleventh Station
Jesus Is Nailed to the Cross
When they reached the place called The Skull, they crucified him there and two criminals also, one on the right, the other on the left. Jesus said, "Father forgive them; they do not know what they are doing." Then they cast lots to share out his clothing.

The people stayed there watching him. As for the leaders, they jeered at him. "He saved others," they said "let him save himself if he is the Christ of God, the Chosen One." The soldiers mocked him too, and when they approached to offer him vinegar they said, "If you are the King of the Jews, save yourself." Above him there was an inscription: "This is the king of the Jews."

One of the criminals hanging there abused him. "Are you not the Christ?" he said. "Save yourself and us as well." But the other spoke up and rebuked him. "Have you no fear of God at all?" he said. "You got the same sentence as he did, but in our case we deserved it: we are paying for what we did. But this man has done nothing wrong. "Jesus," he said "remember me when you come into your kingdom." "Indeed, I promise you," he replied "today you will be with me in paradise."

LUKE 23:33-43

My breath grows weak,
and the gravediggers are gathering for me.
I am the butt of mockers,
and all my waking hours I brood on their spitefulness....
I have become a byword among the people,
and a creature on whose face to spit.
My eyes grow dim with grief,
and my limbs wear away like a shadow.

Pity me, pity me, you my friends,
for the hand of God has struck me.

JOB 17:1-2, 6-7; 19:21

Twelfth Station
Jesus Dies on the Cross
From the sixth hour there was darkness over all the land until the ninth hour. And about the ninth hour, Jesus cried out in a loud voice, *"Eli, Eli, lama sabach-thani?"* that is, "My God, my God, why have you deserted me?" When some of those who stood there heard this, they said, "This man is calling on Elijah," and one of them quickly ran to get a sponge which he dipped in vinegar and, putting it on a reed, gave it him to drink. "Wait!" said the rest of them "and see if Elijah will come to save him." But Jesus, again crying out in a loud voice, yielded up his spirit.

At that, the veil of the Temple was torn in two from top to bottom; the earth quaked; the rocks were split; the tombs opened and the bodies of many holy men rose from the dead, and these, after his resurrection, came out of the tombs, entered the Holy City and appeared to a number of people. Meanwhile the centurion, together with the others guarding Jesus, had seen the earthquake and all that was taking place, and they were terrified and said, "In truth this was a son of God."

MATTHEW 27:45-54

We are only the earthenware jars that hold this treasure, to make it clear that such an overwhelming power comes from God and not from us. We are in difficulties on all sides, but never cornered; we see no answer to our problems, but never despair, we have been persecuted, but never deserted; knocked down, but never killed; always, wherever we may be, we carry with us in our body the death of Jesus, so that the life of Jesus, too, may always be seen in our body. Indeed, while we are still alive, we are consigned to our death every day, for the sake of Jesus, so that in our mortal flesh the life of Jesus, too, may be openly shown. So death is at work in us, but life in you.

2 CORINTHIANS 4:7-12

Thirteenth Station
Jesus Is Taken Down From the Cross
And many women were there watching from a distance, the same women who had followed Jesus from Galilee and looked after him. Among them were Mary of

Magdala, Mary the mother of James and Joseph, and the mother of Zebedee's sons.

When it was evening, there came a rich man of Arimathaea, called Joseph, who had himself become a disciple of Jesus. This man went to Pilate and asked for the body of Jesus. Pilate thereupon ordered it to be handed over.

MATTHEW 27:55-58

God's love for us was revealed
when God sent into the world his only Son
so that we could have life through him;
this is the love I mean:
not our love for God,
but God's love for us
when he sent his Son
to be the sacrifice that takes our sins away.
My dear people,
since God has loved us so much,
we too should love one another.

1 JOHN 4:9-11

Fourteenth Station
Jesus Is Placed in the Sepulchre
It was now evening, and since it was Preparation Day— that is, the day before the Sabbath—there came Joseph of Arimathaea, a prominent member of the Council, who himself lived in the hope of seeing the kingdom of God, and he boldly went to Pilate and asked for the

body of Jesus. Pilate, astonished that he should have died so soon, summoned the centurion and enquired if he had been dead for some time. Having been assured of this by the centurion, he granted the corpse to Joseph who bought a shroud, took Jesus down from the cross, wrapped him in the shroud and laid him in a tomb which had been hewn out of the rock. He then rolled a stone against the entrance to the tomb. Mary of Magdala and Mary the mother of Joset took note of where he was laid.

MARK 15:42-47 NJB

So for anyone who is in Christ, there is a new creation: the old order is gone and a new being is there to see. It is all God's work; he reconciled us to himself through Christ and he gave us the ministry of reconciliation. I mean, God was in Christ reconciling the world to himself, not holding anyone's faults against them, but entrusting to us the message of reconciliation.

So we are ambassadors for Christ; it is as though God were urging you through us, and in the name of Christ we appeal to you to be reconciled to God.

2 CORINTHIANS 5:17-20 NJB

Fifteenth Station
Jesus Is Risen
But Mary was standing outside near the tomb, weeping. Then, as she wept, she stooped to look inside, and saw two angels in white sitting where the body of Jesus

had been, one at the head, the other at the feet. They said, "Woman, why are you weeping?" "They have taken my Lord away," she replied, "and I don't know where they have put him." As she said this she turned round and saw Jesus standing there, though she did not realise that it was Jesus. Jesus said to her, "Woman, why are you weeping? Who are you looking for?" Supposing him to be the gardener, she said, "Sir, if you have taken him away, tell me where you have put him, and I will go and remove him." Jesus said, "Mary!" She turned round then and said to him in Hebrew, "Rabbuni!"— which means Master. Jesus said to her, "Do not cling to me, because I have not yet ascended to the Father. But go to the brothers, and tell them: I am ascending to my Father and your Father, to my God and your God." So Mary of Magdala told the disciples, "I have seen the Lord," and that he had said these things to her.

JOHN 20:11-18 NJB

Now if Christ is proclaimed as raised from the dead, how can some of you be saying that there is no resurrection of the dead? If there is no resurrection of the dead, then Christ cannot have been raised either, and if Christ has not been raised, then our preaching is without substance, and so is your faith. What is more, we have proved to be false witnesses to God, for testifying against God that he raised Christ to life when he did not raise him—if it is true that the dead are not raised. For, if the dead are not raised, neither is Christ; and if Christ has not been raised, your faith is pointless and you have not, after all, been released from your sins. In addition, those who have fallen asleep in Christ are utterly lost. If our hope in Christ has been for this life only, we are of all people the most pitiable.

In fact, however, Christ has been raised from the dead, as the first-fruits of all who have fallen asleep. As it was by one man that death came, so through one man has come the resurrection of the dead. Just as all die in Adam, so in Christ all will be brought to life.

1 CORINTHIANS 15:12-22 NJB

Let us pray
Lord Jesus Christ, you walked the way to Calvary to rescue us from our sin, but the Father, pleased with your obedient submission to his will, glorified you in the resurrection. May we follow obediently in your footsteps so that one day we may share in the glory of your risen life. We make this prayer through you who lives with the Father and Holy Spirit, one God for ever and ever.

The Easter or Paschal Triduum
When Life Conquered Death

Three days leading up to Easter morning—Holy
Thursday, Good Friday, and Holy Saturday night—are
the climax of the whole Christian year. They take us into
the central mystery of our faith, the event by which we
are saved. We speak of these three days as the time in
which we celebrate the paschal mystery, a *mystery*
because God intervenes in human history on our
behalf, and *paschal* because these three days have their
roots in the Jewish Passover (paschal) which celebrated
Israel's deliverance from slavery when they passed over
the Red Sea to freedom. The church sees the Jewish
Passover festival as prefiguring its own deliverance by
the saving power of Christ's resurrection when he
passed over from death to life.

The Jews celebrate the Passover as the greatest feast
of their year. On this feast the Jews, as God had com-
manded, sacrificed a lamb and sprinkled its blood on the
doors of their homes. So it is with us. Our Paschal Lamb
is Christ. When we make our Easter Communion, we
are united with him in his death and "pass over" with
him to resurrection and eternal life. At Easter we eat the
Paschal Lamb as food for our spiritual journey to the
Promised Land. By choosing to give his life for us, Christ
entered the glory of the resurrection to send forth his
Spirit on the church. Christ's loving obedience to his
Father is the source of our salvation.

* * * *

Being as all men are,
[Jesus] was humbler yet,
even to accepting death,
death on a cross.
But God raised him high
and gave him the name
which is above all other names
so that all beings
in the heavens, on earth and in the underworld,
should bend the knee at the name of Jesus
and that every tongue should acclaim
Jesus Christ as Lord,
to the glory of God the Father.

PHILIPPIANS 2:8-11

Bless me, Lord, in this Holy Week, and give me the grace to know your loving presence more intimately.

Henri Nouwen

Father, We Need Your Grace

Holy Father, we praise and thank you that at no time in history did you ever abandon us. Through your Son's passion, death, and resurrection, you changed the old order of sin and overcame our sinfulness. The darkness of despair gave way to the bright light and promise of immortality. You did not refuse us anything you could give, and so you sent your Son among us who gave his life as a ransom that set us free.

We need your grace especially these three days to

help us to appreciate how wonderful you are as our Father.

May we come to know and love you more as we enter into Jesus' offering of his life to you. For our sake may we too offer our lives to you whom we dare to call our Father.

M.B.

Lord Jesus, Be With Me

Lord Jesus, be with me during these three special days when with the church I relive your passion, death, and resurrection. You suffered the intense agony of the cross as a sign not only of your love for your Father, but also of your love for me.

You endured the darkness of desolation not only during your trial and suffering on the cross, but also during your agony in the garden. You felt alone and betrayed by your own people and your chosen disciples. There were few to plead your cause, proclaim your innocence, and support you in your moment of trial, and yet when darkness seemed to engulf you, you were still the Light of the world shining through for all those who believed in you as Brother, Savior, Lord. Make us one with you as once again we relive the three extraordinary days when life conquered death and darkness gave way to the new dawn of Christian hope and joy.

M.B.

Spirit, Give Me Understanding

Spirit of God, fill my mind and heart with a deeper understanding and awareness of God the Father's love for me when, in obedience to his Father's will, his Son gave his life for me. It was the ultimate testimony of his dedication to healing and restoring our fallen condition. May I live again the drama of Jesus' unique sacrifice and enter into the emotions of my Lord and Savior in a way that will change my life. May I see my trials and tribulations as being taken up into my Lord's suffering, death, and resurrection and given their true meaning. Only you can enter my spirit and take me into the mystery of what happened during Holy Week. Be with me now and always.

M.B.

Jesus, My Way, Truth, and Life

Lord Jesus, I love you, and yet I know deep in my heart that I do not love you as I should. Through the Holy Spirit you have called me to follow you, because you are the Way for me. But I have not always kept close to you; I have allowed myself to stray to paths different from yours. You are the Truth in my life; you know me through and through and yet I delude myself with false images of who I am and try to be someone other than who you would have me be. You are my Life and promise me eternal life if I live for you and by your teaching; still I do not grasp what life is all about and do not respond to the challenge and vitality of your gospel. Help me this Holy Week to stay close to you, to know myself better, and to find the value of self-denial in your example and teaching.

M.B.

Mary, Mother of Sorrows

Mary, Mother of Sorrows, by the pain you suffered as you stood by the foot of the cross, be with me as I dedicate myself in these three special days to your Son. May I stand beside you in faith and courage as I try to understand however poorly the extent of your love. May the memory of your motherly love sustain me and encourage me to remain faithful to your Son in any trials that come my way. As I am with you in my sorrow, may I also share your joy in the resurrection that will change and give true direction to my life, through Jesus Christ our Lord.

M.B.

Holy Thursday

Jesus celebrated the Jewish Passover with his apostles. He gave them a new commandment that they love one another as he loved them. This love is shown in service. During the supper Jesus washed the feet of his apostles. He instituted the sacrament of the Eucharist, the Mass, and so placed himself forever at the service of the church. The Mass makes effectively present the events that took place on that night; it is the source from which all the other sacraments flow and toward which they all lead.

* * * *

Remember, the ransom that was paid to free you from the useless way of life your ancestors handed down was not paid in anything corruptible, neither in silver nor gold, but in the precious blood of a lamb without spot or stain, namely Christ, who, though known since before the world was made, has been revealed only in our time, the end of the ages, for your sake.

1 PETER 1:18-20

Lord of lords in human vesture,
In the Body and the Blood
He will give to all the faithful
His own self for heavenly food.

From "Liturgy of Saint James"

O God, who in this wondrous sacrament has left unto us a memorial of your passion, grant us so to venerate the sacred mysteries of your body and blood, that we may ever continue to feel within ourselves the blessed fruit of your redemption.

Saint Thomas Aquinas

I am not worthy, holy Lord,
That you should come to me;
Speak but the word: one gracious word
Can set the sinner free.

H.W. Baker

The Legacy of Love

Jesus, you gave the world a new meaning of the word *love*. You purified it of all self-seeking and self-glorification. The way you lived it is an incomprehensible mystery, because it reaches down into the depths of our being. Your love was oriented to your Father, and you related everything you said and did to him. Your message of complete love was accepted by few during your lifetime, even when you made the supreme sacrifice of your life. Your last words were forgiving those who crucified you and commending your spirit to your Father. Your last meal with your apostles was a love feast in which you spoke of your need to love. Teach us, Lord, to love as you did all whom we meet in our life's journey. Write the word *love* large in our lives, so that in some small way people will see that you live in us. We ask this of you

as we celebrate the special night of your last meal with
your apostles.

M.B.

The Presence of the Lord

Lord Jesus, you loved being human. You came on earth
to show God's love for us. You did not want to leave us
orphans, and so you made your last night on earth a
special occasion for your apostles. At the end of the
great Jewish feast of the Passover, you offered them the
greatest gift of all. You broke bread and blessed wine.
When you gave it to them, you said it was your body
and blood. You told them that whenever they met
together in the future, they were to do the same. In this
way, you would be present to them, as truly as you were
the night of the Last Supper.

We praise and thank you that, down through the
ages, the apostles and those who came after them in the
Church were faithful to your command. The New
Covenant of promise you made to your followers is
your body and blood given to us in the Mass. May we
remember every time we participate in the Mass, that
we share with you as once you shared the Last Supper
with your apostles. May it be for us as it was for you, an
expression of our love for God our Father, who sent
you to share your life with us forever. This is your last
testament and legacy, for which we praise and thank
you.

M.B.

The Legacy of Service

Lord Jesus, even though as God's only Son you were Lord and Master, throughout your life you gave us an unparalleled example of service. One of the last acts of service you performed was washing the feet of your disciples. You told them that they, like you, were called to be servants. Help us to understand that what we do for others is done for and to you. It is in this service and giving without counting the cost that we find you, our neighbor, and ourselves.

M.B.

Good Friday

On this day we celebrate the passion and death of our Lord. Jesus died that we might live, and by his wounds be healed. He transformed the cross of shame into a symbol of triumph. On the cross he offered the perfect prayer of forgiveness for all peoples to the end of time

We join in his sufferings by giving of our lives to him, knowing that if we die with him we will also rise with him. We call this Friday "good" because Christ by his death brought eternal life to all who believe in his name

* * * *

When he died, he died, once for all, to sin, so his life now is life with God; and in that way, you too must consider yourselves to be dead to sin but alive for God in Christ Jesus.

ROMANS 6:10-11

O sacred head, now wounded,
With grief and shame weighed down,
Now scornfully surrounded,
With thorns, thine only crown!
O sacred Head, what glory,
What bliss, till now was thine!
Yet though despised and gory,
I joy to call thee mine.

What thou, my Lord, has suffered
Was all for sinners' gain:
Mine, mine was the transgression,
But thine the deadly pain.
Lo, here I fall, my Savior!
'Tis I deserved thy place;
Look on me with thy favor,
Vouchsafe to me thy grace.

Saint Bernard of Clairvaux

At the cross, her station keeping,
Stood the mournful mother weeping,
Where he hung, the dying Lord;
For her soul of joy bereaved,

Bowed with anguish deeply grieved,
Felt the sharp and piercing sword.

Jesus, may her deep devotion
Stir in me the same emotion.
Fount of love, Redeemer kind:
That my heart fresh ardor gaining;
And a purer love attaining,
May with thee acceptance find.

Stabat Mater,
trans. by Edward Caswall

Thou who was Center of the whole earth on Calvary, reign over north and south, east and west.

Christina Rossetti

Correct Use of Suffering
Heavenly Father, teach us the lessons of Good Friday and why Jesus, our Lord and Savior, died for our sake. Give us the grace to know that he did not die to save us from suffering, which is, and always will be, part of our lives, but that when we unite our sufferings with his we will understand more clearly his love for you and for us. Through your Holy Spirit, remind us that Jesus died that we might live as he lived here on earth—not for ourselves alone, but for others even when, like Christ on the cross, it causes us pain.

M.B.

The Price of Our Redemption

God our Father, we praise and thank you that on Good Friday your beloved Son Jesus paid the ultimate price, giving his life as a witness to his love for you. Being one like us and yet divine, he could restore our dignity and destiny. We praise you that you heard his prayer on the cross; in forgiving the soldiers who crucified him and the priests and people who mocked him, you also forgave us our many faults and failings. We thank you for your loving presence to Jesus in his agony, which is also our consolation that you will never desert us in our moments of trial and tribulation. Grant that on this day and throughout our lives we will appreciate how precious was the price of our redemption.

M.B.

Inner Peace in Suffering

Lord Jesus Christ, who showed us that the path to selfless love and the pain of rejection by those near to us may often lead to the cross, give us your grace of inner peace, courage, and forgiveness for those who hurt us. Help us to understand that love such as yours costs nothing less than everything.

M.B.

The Cross as the Blessing of Jesus

Holy Spirit, keep my eyes fixed on the cross that I kissed today as a sign of my love for Jesus my Savior. May I realize the extent to which sin will drive men to torture and kill even innocent people. Enlighten my spirit that, sad though today's events have been, they help me to realize that love divine has no limits for those who are children of God our Father. Whenever and wherever I see the cross, may I bless and revere Jesus who gave his life for me and did not count the cost.

M.B.

Suffering Is Redemptive

Heavenly Father, in a mysterious way your dying Son Jesus showed the value of suffering. For him it was a sign of his love for you, which transformed suffering and gave it a new meaning. In all his pain he did not lose his inner peace and belief that you were with him and that his suffering had a purpose.

Be with us today and all through our lives. Give us the grace to unite all our sufferings with his, so that in some way we share with him in the redemption of our world. Make it a source of a closer relationship with you, so that we see you as our Father who will not cause needless suffering. May we look beyond the darkness of suffering to the light and glory of the resurrection.

M.B.

Suffering Helps Us to Heal

Holy Spirit, we pray for wisdom and insight to discern that suffering works mysteriously in our lives. It helps us to identify with and be a source of healing for other sufferers, as our compassion speaks to them in ways "beyond words." From our own experience of pain, we reach out and begin to see our suffering as a blessing for others because we are able to heal only insofar as we are wounded. May Christ who healed us by his wounds be with us in our suffering, as we reach out to him and to all we meet who need compassion and healing.

M.B.

Holy Saturday

This night of Passover, when Christ passed from death to the glory of the resurrection, is the most important moment in the liturgical year. In it we also celebrate our own passing over from sin and death to newness of life in the risen Lord. From the earliest times, Christians devoted this night of the resurrection to watching and waiting. As faithful people we keep the lamp of our faith alight so that when Christ emerges from the tomb he will find us awake and ready to celebrate his victory. The resurrection of the Lord Jesus is the climax of history toward which God our Father has been directing us from the beginning of time.

* * * *

The love of God will rise before the sun.

Gary Ault

'Tis thine own third morning! Rise, O buried Lord!

Loose the souls long prisoned, bound with Satan's
    chain;
All that now is fallen raise to life again;
Show thy face in brightness, bid the nations see;
Bring again our daylight: Day returns with thee!

"Welcome, happy morning!" age to age shall say:
Hell today is vanquished, heaven is won today.
Lo! The dead is living, God forevermore.
'Tis thine own third morning. Rise, O buried Lord.

Venantius Fortunatus,
trans. by John Ellerton

Light Out of Darkness

Heavenly Father, we praise you on this blessed night
when you dispelled the darkness of death with the
bright light of the resurrection of your Son Jesus Christ.
The Easter candle that we light this night reminds us of
the new dawn of hope—our sins washed away in the living waters of baptism.

Tonight as we welcome new members into our
family, may we be reminded of our own baptism. May
we be renewed again in our love and commitment to
you through Jesus Christ our Lord.

M.B.

A New Creation

Heavenly Father, we thank you that in the Easter vigil we celebrate the new creation when the whole of your original creation from the beginning of time was taken up and renewed in the resurrection of your Son. His resurrection heals us and our world damaged by sin, and in his rising we emerge from the tomb of death into the womb of life where we are reborn as children of the light. Our lives are transformed by your Son's resurrection, which gives us a new vision of everything around us as we follow him who is the light of the world. May we walk in this light for the rest of our lives, until we reach our longed-for home with you.

M.B.

The Victory Over Death

Lord Jesus, we cannot find words to express our wonder and thanksgiving for your great gift of eternal life. When you walked out of your tomb, you left death behind you—this was symbolized in the limp bandages with which your loved ones had wrapped your lifeless body. Ever since, death has lost its victory over us. Your death has brought us new life in a way that was not possible without your suffering for our sake.

All seemed lost to your followers as you lay in the darkness, silence, and seeming finality of your tomb until you gave them new hope on the dawn of Easter Sunday when you emerged triumphant to share your new life with them and us.

In the future when the days seem dark to us and we cannot cope with our problems, may we think of you and your resurrection; may it always be our hope that nothing, even death itself, will ever finally overcome us.

M.B.

The Holy Spirit of Light

Holy Spirit, you have made our minds and hearts aware of what this holy night's vigil means to us and all Christians. We know that through the new life of grace, we have left behind us the death and darkness of sin. We are still wounded by sin, but you have taught us that through the power of Christ's resurrection we will emerge into the new light of day; you have taught us that nothing can ever separate us totally from God the Father's love. In this spirit of confidence and hope, we pray that your Light will lead us kindly, so that our feet walk the right path, which Jesus our Way has trod on our journey back to the Father.

M.B.

Easter Season
A Season of New Life

Easter Sunday

In its earliest days the church held no feasts at all but celebrated only the resurrection, every Sunday of the year. In time Easter Sunday became the preeminent resurrection celebration. In the risen Christ we proclaim that we are a new creation. In and through Christ the whole purpose of creation is fulfilled. We are an Easter people, and alleluia is our song.

* * * *

Easter Blessing

May the glad dawn of Easter morn bring joy to thee.

May the calm eve of Easter leave a peace divine with thee.

May Easter night on thine heart write: O Christ, I live for thee.

Author Unknown

Faith in Life, Not Death

Holy Spirit, we live in a world obsessed by death, so that many give little credence to another form of life beyond the grave. They see personal fulfillment and happiness in terms of financial and material success. The pursuit for success saps so much energy that they have little time for reflection on true Christian values. It is not easy to believe without being unduly influenced by such an environment.

Enlarge our vision, so we can see beyond the present into the future. Let our belief in the resurrection be a witness to all as a sign of our Christian faith.

M.B.

Called to a New Life in the Risen Lord
Heavenly Father, we thank you that you sent your Son Jesus to share completely in our human condition. In his human life you showed your love for us, and even when Jesus died you did not withdraw your love from us. You gave him back to us, so that we could share in his risen life in a new and more glorious way. You transformed his shameful death into victory, so that through his resurrection we are called to the new life of grace. As part of the human race, we sinned against you by crucifying your Son who still bears the wounds of his passion, though now they are signs of victory in his glorified body. You have forgiven us more than we ever could imagine, and through the risen Lord we will always praise you that life, not death, is your calling for your followers.

M.B.

Belief in the Resurrection
Lord Jesus, when you went to comfort your friends Martha and Mary on the death of their brother Lazarus, Martha reminded you that if you had come sooner, her brother might not have died. As you assured her that those who believe in you will never die, you also

restored physical life to her brother. Restore us, Lord, to a new life in you so that we never cease to believe that no matter what difficulties and trials we have to endure, we will always believe that with you we will overcome them because of our belief in your resurrection.

Lord, without this central belief in your resurrection, we would be the most unfortunate people in the world. You are the only one who has come back from the dead by your own power, and our belief in the world to come depends entirely on your word and the testimony of those who saw you after your resurrection. Our belief in the after-life will never be easy for us, because it is beyond the boundaries of our human understanding and experience. We have to believe it as a mystery of faith. On this Easter Day when we celebrate your resurrection, we pray that you will send your Holy Spirit to strengthen our faith. Like the apostle Thomas, we seem to need physical proof of your resurrection. But you said that those are blessed who have not seen and yet believe.

Lord, on this day of days as I profess my belief in your resurrection, help my unbelief.

M.B.

Dead to Sin

Holy Spirit, since through baptism we share in the risen life of Jesus Christ, help us to die to sin and live the new life of grace. This will never be easy, because we live in a damaged world and are wounded in body and spirit. When we fall, lift us up again. Help us to keep our eyes fixed on the risen Lord who conquered sin and death for our sake. With this belief and hope, we know that all will be well in our lives.

M.B.

Risen Jesus Conquers All Fear

Lord Jesus, our Life and Hope, we praise you that nothing could keep you forever in your grave. You overcame death because you are Life itself. You overcame death to share your risen life with us. As we celebrate your resurrection on Easter Day, help us to remember that we should not be afraid of anything, even death itself, because you are always with us to support us and give us hope that life in you will never end.

M.B.

The Ascension of Our Lord
Thursday of the Sixth Week of Easter

Christ's Ascension is our guarantee that one day we will be with him in heaven to praise the glory of God our Father. The Ascension is our hope of the great inheritance that awaits those who believe in the power of the risen Christ.

* * * *

Lord, in the morning thou shalt hear
My voice ascending high;
To thee will I direct my prayer,
To thee lift up mine eye.

Up to the hills where Christ is gone,
To plead for all his saints;
Presenting, at the Father's throne,
Our songs and our complaints.

Isaac Watts

You Will Take Us to Your Home

Lord Jesus Christ, I praise you as we commemorate your return to your Father's home to assume the glory you had before you came among us as a baby. May we always look upward in hope, waiting for the day when you will return to your world, where death and sadness will be no more. Let your Holy Spirit always remind us that you have won the victory in which we all share and that one day you will take us to your home, never again to part from you and those whom we have loved while here on earth.

M.B.

Still Our Friend

Lord Jesus, I praise and adore you in your risen and ascended life with the Father to whom you gave your whole life, even to enduring the pain and shame of crucifixion. I thank you that because of your love for us, you retain your glorified human body; this helps me remember that you are still my friend, even though I cannot see you with my human eyes. I believe that you still watch over our daily personal lives as you promised you would. You have not left us orphans, and we feel so at one with you that in a special way we share with you new life in heaven. Be with us in our good times as well as bad, so that, no matter what happens, we will continue to believe that you are as present with us today as you were when you lived on earth.

M.B.

Sharing Our Inheritance

Lord Jesus, you left your Father's home to share with us on earth. You were prepared to be as humble as a servant and accepted without complaint the taunts, insults, indifference, and betrayal of your own people. You knew that the most important thing in life was to do your Father's will, and this you did perfectly even in surrendering to a violent death. Give us courage to live as you did, so that we will see everything we suffer as part of the price we willingly pay if we are to enter into our inheritance where you will share your risen and ascended life with us.

M.B.

Ascended Jesus Our Hope

Holy Spirit, even though the ascended Jesus has passed beyond our sight—not to abandon us but to be our hope—give us a desire to be with him, a desire that will encourage us to live our lives as he did. Just as he once wished to be with us on earth, may we long to be with him who is our Hope and Fulfillment. This will give us the extra spiritual strength to overcome temptation.

M.B.

Pentecost Sunday
The Age of Spiritual Renewal

Today we celebrate the coming of the Holy Spirit to the fledgling church gathered in an upper room in Jerusalem.

We live in the last age of the church, which is called the age of the Holy Spirit. As Christians, we must proclaim that God is our Father, and that Jesus is Lord. We cannot do this until we receive the Holy Spirit. All true prayer within us comes through the indwelling of the Holy Spirit and it is he who takes all our needs to the Father.

* * * *

You will receive power when the Holy Spirit comes on you, and then you will be my witnesses not only in Jerusalem but throughout Judaea and Samaria, and indeed to the ends of the earth.

ACTS 1:8

Happy the man whose words come from the Holy Spirit and not from himself.

Saint Anthony of Padua

Lord God, the Holy Ghost!
In this accepted hour,
As on the day of Pentecost,
Descend in all your power.

James Montgomery

Breathe on me, Breath of God,
Fill me with life anew,
That I may love what thou dost love,
And do what thou wouldst do.

Breathe on me, Breath of God,
Until my heart is pure:
Until with thee I have one will
To do and to endure.

Breathe on me, Breath of God,
Till I am wholly thine,
Until this earthly part of me
Glows with thy fire divine.

Breathe on me, Breath of God,
So shall I never die,
But live with thee the perfect life
Of thine eternity.

Edwin Hatch

Spirit of God, descend upon my heart....
I ask no dream, no prophet ecstasies,
No sudden rending of the veil of clay,
No angel visitant, no opening skies;
But take the dimness of my soul away.

George Croly

Prayer to the Holy Spirit

As the wind is thy symbol
so forward our goings.
As the dove
so launch us heavenwards.
As water
so purify our spirits.
As a cloud
so abate our temptations.
As dew
so revive our languor.
As fire
so purge out our dross.

Christina Rossetti

The Coming of the Holy Spirit

Holy Spirit, we give you thanks that on this day we
remember that you came upon Mary the mother of
Jesus, the holy women, and the apostles waiting in the
upper room; you gave them special gifts by which they
were no longer afraid to publicly proclaim the risen
Christ and so begin the great mission of the church that

will persevere until the end of time. I thank you that you have come to me, lifting me up when I was spiritually low, giving me hope in moments of despair, joy in periods of sadness, and teaching me how to pray when I could not find words to express my deepest feelings. Abide with me, Spirit, as I look forward to Christ's return.

M.B.

The Gift of Love

Holy Spirit, the greatest gift you give us is the Spirit of love which changes our whole attitude. It is a gift that will endure throughout eternity. Teach me how to love God as my Father who loves me more than I love myself. Unless and until I love myself, I shall never be able to love anyone, because true love of self is the basis of all human relationships. May I exclude no one from this love, especially those who have hurt me or offended me in any way.

M.B.

An End to Fear

Holy Spirit, we thank you that you inspire us to approach God not as his slaves but as his children. We must never allow fear to control us. Fear loses its hold over us when we turn to you for guidance and help. You teach us to live by the words of Jesus when he told us that God loves us more than any human father and that he will give us all we need if we seek above everything else his kingdom of love and peace.

Teach us to seek this kingdom in all we say and do, so that our lives may bear witness to it.

M.B.

The Fatherhood of God

Holy Spirit, you came to us at our baptism and made us Christians. You guide us all so that we live faithful to our Christian vocation. And you confirmed in us the vision of God as Father, which Jesus preached. This gift gives us the freedom, friendship, and familiarity to call God by the affectionate name of Abba Father. We praise you that we are the adopted sons and daughters of God whom we dare to call our Father.

M.B.

The Gift of Peace

Holy Spirit, I pray this day for the gift of inner peace. We all say we want inner peace, but are afraid to pay the price that such deep peace demands of us. I yearn to discover within myself the meaning of full gospel peace, but often I close my mind and heart to what it really means. To understand the meaning of peace, I know I have to reflect on the peace of Jesus himself and, like him, appreciate the suffering and upheaval it will cause in my life. He said that peacemakers will be called children of God. I want to be a peace lover and a peacemaker. Holy Spirit, you alone can change me and bring the peace I ask.

M.B.

Christian Unity

Father, we praise and thank you for our Christian faith, which is your gift to us. Bless all Christians of all denominations who pray, work, and strive for unity and continue their work of bridge-building. We are all enriched by one another's gifts and ministries, and the source of these is the Holy Spirit who transforms our set attitudes of religion into a living faith whose witness the world needs if it is to believe in the power and resurrection of your Son Jesus Christ.

M.B.

Trinity Sunday
Sunday After Pentecost

The Trinity is a mystery of one God in three divine Persons about which we never would have known had it not been revealed to us by Jesus Christ. We ascribe different functions to the Father, Son, and Holy Spirit, all equal in power. The Father is seen as the Creator, the Son as the Savior or Redeemer, and the Spirit as the Sanctifier. When we praise one we do so to all, because prayer takes us into the heart of the blessed Trinity. If we, like Jesus, model our lives on the Trinity, the God of love, peace, and holiness will be with us.

* * * *

Holy Father, holy Son,
Holy Spirit, three we name thee.
While in essence only one,
Undivided God, we claim thee;
And, adoring, bend the knee,
While we own the mystery.

Spare thy people, Lord, we pray,
By a thousand snares surrounded;
Keep us without sin today;
Never let us be confounded.
Lo, I put my trust in thee,
Never, Lord, abandon me.

Clarence Walworth

Holy, holy, holy!
Lord God almighty!
Early in the morning
Our song shall rise to thee:
Holy, holy, holy!
Merciful and mighty!
God in three Persons,
Blessed Trinity!

Reginald Heber

I bind unto myself today
The strong name of the Trinity,
By invocation of the same,
The Three in One, the One in Three.
Of whom all nature hath creation,

Eternal Father, Spirit, Word:
Praise to the Lord of my salvation,
Salvation is of Christ the Lord.

Saint Patrick,
trans. by Cecil Frances Alexander

Come, Holy Ghost, with God the Son
And God the Father, ever one:
Shed forth thy grace within our breast,
And dwell with us, a ready guest.

O Father, that we ask be done,
Through Jesus Christ, thine only Son,
Who, with the Holy Ghost and thee,
Doth live and reign eternally.

Saint Ambrose,
trans. by John M. Neale

Glory be to God the Father,
Glory be to God the Son,
Glory be to God the Spirit,
Great Jehovah, Three in One.
Praise from all in earth and heaven
Unto thee be ever given,
Holy, blessed Trinity!

H.A. Martin

Our Mission in the Trinity

Jesus said to his disciples, "All authority in heaven and on earth has been given to me. Go, therefore, make disciples of all nations; baptise them in the name of the Father and of the Son and of the Holy Spirit" (Mt 28:18-19 NJB).

His command to preach his gospel is given in the name of the blessed Trinity. In faith we adore God our Father, who sent Jesus, his Word, to bring us truth and his Spirit to make us holy. We will never understand the Trinity, a mystery beyond our limits, and so we accept it in faith. When our life on earth is over, we will live within ourselves the life of the Trinity for all eternity. We pray for this gift of faith in the name of the Father, Son, and Holy Spirit.

M.B.

Spirit of Truth

Holy Spirit of Truth, enlighten our minds and hearts, so that through your grace we may be taken more deeply into an awareness of the truth about God.

M.B.

Corpus Christi
Sunday After Trinity Sunday

In people and events, Christ is present to us in many ways. We Catholics believe he is also present in our churches in a unique way. It is this special presence that we celebrate in today's feast. The words *Corpus Christi* mean *body of Christ,* and we believe that the risen Jesus is as truly present on our altars under the form of bread as he was when he lived on earth in his human form.

* * * *

Godhead here in hiding,
Whom I do adore,
Masked by these bare shadows,
Shape and nothing more,
See, Lord, at thy service
Low lies here a heart
Lost, all lost in wonder
At the God thou art.

Jesu, whom I look at
Shrouded here below,
I beseech thee send me
What I long for so,
Some day to gaze on thee
Face to face in light
And be blest forever
With thy glory's sight.

Saint Thomas Aquinas,
trans. by Gerard Manley Hopkins, S.J.

Bread of heaven,
Feed me till I want no more.

William Williams

O gentle Father ... I beg of you that you will do mercy to the world and to the holy church....

Give them then the Bread of Life, that is, the fruit of the blood of your Son, which they ask of you for the praise and glory of your name and the salvation of souls.

Saint Catherine of Siena

Lord Jesus, I praise and thank you that you stay with us in the Blessed Sacrament. I kneel before you, Lord. There is so much I want to say, but words could not express my emotions. I need you so deeply that it is best for me to be silent and just look at you there with love, poor though it is, in my heart. You know me through and through, and from you there is no hiding place. I just want to be here with you as honestly as I can. I know you want me to love myself, but this is not possible without your Holy Spirit. I want to be as nothing before you, so that you may clothe me with your love and gentleness. In the silence, Lord, you will speak so I just kneel here and listen. Thank you.

M.B.

The Sacred Heart of Jesus
Third Friday After Pentecost Sunday

Jesus' love for each one of us heals us and reconciles us to God our Father. No one loves us as he does, and to prove this he gave his life for us. The Good Shepherd that he is, he will not abandon us, and he constantly looks for the sheep who have strayed. He watches over the whole of our lives, and this is why we have a very special devotion to his Sacred Heart, which is the symbol and center of love. Jesus puts his new heart in us so that we return love for love.

* * * *

Lord Jesus, who in your humanity loved God our Father so perfectly that you gave your life for us, we praise and thank you for what you did for us during your time among us on earth. You have given us the gift of inner peace; no matter what unexpected storms threaten the frail craft of our mortal bodies, you are forever with us calming the waters and giving us the security of peace. May the Holy Spirit make us constantly aware that you alone are our Servant-King, teaching us that love is the fulfilling of the law. May our love for our neighbors and ourselves reflect the love you have for us and for God our Father. Sacred Heart of Jesus, I place all my trust in you.

M.B.

Our Need of Christ's Message of Love

Father, we praise you that you sent your Son among us to be an example of how we should live. His love for us reflects your love. We pray that we will open our hearts to him, so that we bring his loving message to those we meet. Make us aware of the need of your Son in a world that seems to have forgotten the gospel of love and forgiveness. May we live and proclaim his message so that your kingdom may come on earth.

M.B.

Unity With the Wounded Christ

Lord Jesus, even though you gave yourself completely in the service of everyone, you were crucified by those who should have known who you were and understood your simple message of love. The night of your betrayal and trial, you said that your soul was "sorrowful to the point of death" (Mk 14:34 NJB) at the prospect of what would happen to you. May I stay with you, Lord, to comfort you and never leave your side. I am weak but you will make me strong. Teach me to love you as you deserve, and may my dedication to you ease the pain of your wounded heart.

M.B.

Healing as Jesus Healed

Lord Jesus, you saw the image of your Father in everyone, especially the sick, poor, and underprivileged for whom you said you came. You spoke to them and

touched them, so that they were healed and saw, perhaps for the first time, a purpose in their lives. Grant
that our love of you may shine through to those who
come to us for help and healing. As we touch them,
may they realize that it is you, living in us, who makes
them whole.

M.B.

Christ the King
Last Sunday in Ordinary Time

God the Father looks after his sheep through Jesus
Christ his Shepherd and King. By human standards, a
king is associated with wealth and power, but Christ's
kingdom is not of this world. He is a spiritual Leader
whose sovereignty will never pass away, because he
reigns in people's hearts. He is the Servant-King who
suffered for his people whom he came on earth to set
free. We follow his example by trying to love and serve
God in people.

* * * *

There is no King but him whom I worship and adore.
Were I to be killed a thousand times for my allegiance
to him, I should still go on as I have begun. I should
still be his man. Christ is on my lips, Christ is in my
heart; no torments can take him from me.

Genesius, early Roman martyr

The kingdom of God is simply God's power enthroned
in our hearts and what Christian joy is all about.

John Main, Benedictine monk

Teach me, my God and King,
In all things thee to see,
And what I do in anything,
To do it as for thee.

George Herbert

Alleluia! King eternal,
Thee the Lord of lords we own;
Alleluia! Born of Mary,
Earth thy footstool, heaven thy throne.

Alleluia! Sing to Jesus!
His the scepter, his the throne;
Alleluia! His the triumph,
His the victory alone.

William Chatterton Dix

Jesus, our everlasting King,
Accept the tribute which we bring;
Accept thy well-deserved renown,
And wear our praises as thy crown.

Isaac Watts

The Humble and the Kingdom

Heavenly Father, even though your Son was divine like you and the Ruler over all rulers, he still came among us as a humble servant. Wise men from the East looking for a king asked King Herod where he could be found, never expecting that it would be in a stable and not a palace. King of the universe, Jesus became the Servant of all, and his message of your kingdom was of love, justice, and peace which he came to establish on earth.

He did this through the service of others rather than through the trappings of secular power. He said your kingdom was not of this world, because it was hidden in people's hearts. You raised him high and crowned him King in his glorified humanity.

As we celebrate his kingship today, may we remember and live by his message, that the poor in spirit, the humble, will inherit the kingdom of heaven.

May your kingdom come in our lives by our humble service in the name and for the sake of Christ, our Lord and King.

M.B.

Preparing for the Second Coming

Holy Spirit, we await the second coming of Christ our Lord when he will gather his people from the four corners of the earth and be seen for who he is. Son of God, he was born to be King not of a temporal power but of an eternal spiritual kingdom. When the last day comes, we shall understand in a more perfect way the Father's plan for our lives and world. Christ will be King of our hearts, and all our eternal joys will be due to the humanity Jesus assumed so he could be the servant of all. Help us to prepare for this day by living as our humble King did while on earth. It is only the humble who will inherit the kingdom.

M.B.

King of Hearts

Lord Jesus, it is hard for me to understand the manner in which you are a King. I believe that your kingship will never pass away nor will your empire ever be destroyed, because your power comes from your divinity. You are the King of hearts, and I love you because your life and message have captured me. I want to be loyal to all you stand for and always feel privileged to call myself a Christian, a follower of you, my King, Brother, and Friend.

M.B.

Welcome Your Kingdom

Heavenly Father, make us so open to your Son's love for us that we welcome with joy the coming of your kingdom in our lives like hungry and grateful children taking bread from his generous sensitive hands, for he knows and fulfills all our needs even before we ask him in prayer.

M.B.

Part 2

Prayers for Special Feasts

The Solemnity of Mary, Mother of God
January 1

We begin the calendar year within the season of Christmas with a special feast of Our Lady. At the Council of Ephesus she was proclaimed the Mother of God, and on this feast we renew our prayers to her for her help and guidance throughout the forthcoming year. She who protected Jesus in his childhood years and stayed with him at the foot of his cross remains with us as our spiritual mother all through our lives.

* * * *

I greet you, Mother of Graces!...

  With the whole Church I profess and proclaim that Jesus Christ in this mystery is the only mediator between God and man: for his incarnation brought to Adam's sons, who are subjected to the power of sin and death, redemption and justification. At the same time, I am deeply convinced [that] no one has been called to participate so deeply as you, the Mother of the Redeemer, in this immense and extraordinary mystery. And no one is better able than you alone, Mary, to let us penetrate this mystery more easily and clearly—we who announce it and form a part of it.

Pope John Paul II

Mother of Christ, Mother of Christ,
Come with thy Babe to me;
Though the world be cold, my heart shall hold
A shelter for him and for thee.

A Notre Dame Hymn

Prayer for Mothers

Lord Jesus, you said suffer little children to come unto you, for of such was the kingdom of heaven. As a young boy, you experienced the unique relationship between mother and child. Once your mother sought after you, worrying until she found you in the temple—three days lost. You understand that mothers do not always know how to cope with their children. They need our prayerful support. We pray for all mothers everywhere, that they may know what it means to love their children—holding them close even as they grow up and grow independent. May mothers and their children together grow in wisdom before God their Father as they imitate the example you set at your home in Nazareth.

M.B.

The Presentation of the Lord
February 2

Forty days after we celebrated the joyful feast of the birthday of our Lord, we recall the day on which he was presented in the temple, to fulfill the law of Moses. Led by the Spirit, Simeon and Anna in the temple recognized and proclaimed with joy Jesus as their Lord. Their long years of waiting for the Messiah were over. Candles are blessed on this day before Mass, and we, like Simeon and Anna, come into our church to proclaim our faith in Christ as the Light of the world. As Christians we are to bring this light of faith to all we meet.

* * * *

Simeon's Prayer

Now, Master, you are letting your servant go in peace
   as you promised;
for my eyes have seen the salvation
which you have made ready in the sight of the nations;
a light of revelation for the gentiles
and glory for your people Israel.

LUKE 2:29-32 NJB

Sharing Jesus With Others

Mary, Mother of Jesus, you gave us an example of perfect obedience when you presented your infant in the temple. According to the law of Moses, all women had to be purified after childbirth; even though it was not necessary for you because of your unique privilege of motherhood and virginity, you gladly obeyed the law in a spirit of gratitude and joy.

Because of your obedience, Simeon and Anna, who had long awaited the Messiah, were able to hold your baby in their arms and see him as the fulfillment of their dreams and hopes. On this special day we celebrate your happiness as you shared your Son with them. Encourage us to share your Son and his message of peace with everyone, so that all may experience the supreme joy of meeting Jesus. May he become for them the fulfilment of their lives.

M.B.

Light of People

Lord Jesus, you are the Light of the world, and on this day we light candles as a sign that you are the Source of our joy and meaning in our lives. May we by our example be a light to others, so that they might find their way to you, and once having found you, may they never let you go. Whenever we light a candle, may we remember someone who needs a prayer, especially if that person no longer attends church or prays to you.

M.B.

Saint Joseph
March 19

Joseph, husband of the Virgin Mary, gives us a perfect example of that special faith through which one is open to whatever God asks. By his openness to God, Joseph reminds us that many great things are achieved even without our knowledge, if we just trust that God our Father is always faithful to his promises.

* * * *

May Saint Joseph become for all of us an exceptional teacher in the service of Christ's saving mission, a mission which is the responsibility of each and every member of the Church: husbands and wives, parents, those who live by the work of their hands or by any other kind of work, those called to the contemplative life, and those called to the active apostolate.

This just man, who bore within himself the entire heritage of the Old Covenant, was also brought into the beginning of the New and Eternal Covenant in Jesus Christ. May he show us the paths of this saving Covenant as we stand at the threshold of the next millennium, in which there must be a continuation and further development of the "fullness of time" that belongs to the ineffable mystery of the Incarnation of the Word.

May Saint Joseph obtain for the church and for the world, as well as for each of us, the blessing of the Father, Son, and Holy Spirit.

Pope John Paul II

Protector of the Family

Joseph, you were uniquely privileged to be chosen by God as the husband of Mary and guardian of Jesus. You were always there for them when they needed you; for us you are the perfect example of someone who fosters security. Your gentleness is evident in the fact that you always stayed in the background. Yet you had the courage to undertake the hazardous journey into Egypt, to protect Mary and her infant Son. Be with us with your spirit of gentleness, responsibility, and courage, so that we, like you, may learn to love and protect those whom God has committed to our care. Be with us today as we celebrate your feast. May we grow in our love for Mary and Jesus.

M.B.

Faith to Say Yes to God

Joseph, you and your wife Mary were completely open and attuned to God's will for you even when it was beyond the range of your human understanding. Mary accepted God's will for her and remained a virgin; you believed the angel's message to you and acted upon it immediately. Your faith, like Mary's, acknowledged that nothing was impossible to God. Pray that I may willingly, immediately, and joyfully accept whatever God wills for me in my life, even though I may not fully understand its consequences. Like you and Mary, may I always say yes to God.

M.B.

The Annunciation of the Lord
March 25

At the Annunciation, Mary said yes to God and by the Holy Spirit conceived the Savior of the world. We too are called to say yes to God in our daily lives. In this way Christ lives in us.

* * * *

When the angel announced to Mary the coming of Christ, she only posed a question: she could not understand how she could take back the gift of herself that she had made to God. The angel explained it, and she understood immediately. Her lips uttered a beautiful response that asserted all that she was as a woman: "I am the servant of the Lord. Let it be done to me as you say."

Mother Teresa

Blessings of a Simple Faith

Mary, our Queen and Mother, we praise you for the simplicity of faith that showed all through your life. You were so in love with God your Father that you dedicated everything to him, even the most precious gift of being a mother. To show your love for him, you were willing to forgo the possibility of becoming the mother of the Messiah, which was the hope of Jewish women of your time. You regarded yourself as privileged just to be the Lord's "lowly handmaid." But God your Father looked on you as someone so special that he chose you as the vessel to contain the most precious gift of Jesus, his only Son. With you as our model, we celebrate on this great feast day your virtue of simplicity of faith. Like you, may we always be open to God's will for us, even though we may not understand where it will lead us. You praised God your Father, because you believed that nothing was impossible to him. May we have your simplicity of faith as we surrender our lives to our loving Father and trust our future to him.

M.B.

Inspiration of the Holy Spirit

Holy Spirit, we thank you that you came upon Mary and inspired her to say yes to the angel Gabriel when he told her that God the Father had chosen her to be the mother of his Son. Throughout her life in all her joys and sorrows, you were her inspiration. Be with us today and always; give us the insight you gave to Mary to discern what God's will is for us and to follow it in faith and trust.

M.B.

Gift of Humility

Mary, teach us to be humble as you were. Your Son Jesus emptied himself of his power and glory when he took flesh in your womb and became a servant to all. He taught us that those who are humble and seem to be least and last in the world's eyes are in fact the greatest and first in God's kingdom. Pray for us, that like you we may become humble and seek God's will in all we say and do. It is only when we come humbly before the Lord that he can do good and great things to and through us.

M.B.

Saint Peter and Saint Paul, Apostles
June 29

Christ promised to remain forever with his church through the apostle Peter, whom he called "the rock" of his church, against which the forces of evil will never triumph. Paul, the great missionary, was the apostle of the Gentiles, spreading the gospel of Christ into Asia and Europe. Through them both, we celebrate the faith and missionary zeal of the followers of Christ.

* * * *

May We, Like Them, Be Witnesses
Holy Spirit, we praise you that you filled Peter and Paul with faith and made them aware of the gospel truth. They dedicated their lives to preaching the good news to people who didn't know or grasp the meaning of the life, death, and resurrection of Jesus the Christ. Through them and their successors, the gospel has been preached and the light of Christ has burned brightly

through the ages. May we, like them, be witnesses to
our Christian faith and spread the word to all we meet.

M.B.

Send Us Your Spirit

Lord Jesus Christ, we praise and thank you that you
chose Peter, a simple fisherman, to be the head of the
apostles. We can identify with him at your trial; though
we love you, we have often failed to witness to our faith
in you; when challenged, we have been afraid to stand
up and be counted for our belief. Send your Holy Spirit
to us as once you sent the Spirit to Peter, so that we may
proclaim that you are the Messiah and Lord of our lives
and world.

M.B.

Saint Peter's Faith

Heavenly Father, we thank you for giving Saint Peter
the great gift of faith in the divinity of Jesus your Son.
We thank you that as leader of the apostles, Peter proclaimed that Jesus was the Christ, and it was upon this
faith that the risen Lord built his church. He gave Saint
Peter the keys of his kingdom of heaven, against which
the evil powers of the world would not prevail. We
thank you for the life, death, and witness of this great
apostle of faith, whom Jesus chose to be a fisher of men
and the leader of his church on earth. May we, like him,
by the way we live bear witness to the divinity of Christ
and the truth of the church he founded on Saint Peter.

M.B.

The Vision of Your Spirit

Lord Jesus Christ, when you appeared to Paul on his journey to Damascus, you changed his whole life. From being a persecutor of your followers, he became an apostle of the gospel. Having been known for his hatred of you, he suffered suspicion from many of your followers, though ultimately he died as a martyr. May we, like him, receive the vision of your Spirit and see more clearly our mission to preach your gospel in season and out of season, so that others may believe and live by your good news of love, peace, and forgiveness.

M.B.

The Transfiguration of the Lord
August 6

At Jesus' transfiguration, Peter, James, and John beheld his glory as Messiah and the fulfillment of the law and the prophets. This extraordinary revealing of Christ's divinity shining through his humanity was so awesome that the disciples were struck down by fear. Just as Jesus helped them to overcome their fear, he also encourages us through our own experiences of his presence to look forward to sharing his glory in heaven with him.

* * * *

O Father, with the eternal Son,
And Holy Spirit, ever One,
Vouchsafe to bring us by thy grace
To see thy glory face to face.

John M. Neale

Sharing Ourselves With Others

Lord Jesus, you shared the events of your public life
with your apostles. Like you, may we share our lives
with others in a spirit of true Christian friendship.

You let them see your sorrow in Gethsemane when
your sweat became as drops of blood. You also let them
see the glory of your transfiguration, when your face
shone like the sun. They had seen you work countless
miracles and heard you claim that God was your Father,
but yet you had not previously allowed your divinity to
shine through; in physical form you were still to them
"just Jesus."

Thank you, not only for your complete sharing with
them, but also for the many times in prayer and in daily
events when we have been aware of your divine presence with us. Shine through us, Lord, in the good and
bad times, so that we will never forget that you are
God's Son and our Friend and compassionate Leader.

M.B.

Believing in Awe and Not Fear

Lord Jesus, your three apostles Peter, James, and John
were so awed at your transfiguration that they were

filled with fear. You were sensitive to their feelings and told them not to be afraid because it was "only you." Our faith in you as God's only Son fills us at times with fears because of the magnitude of what we believe. When we are tempted to feel afraid of the God in you, teach us to love you without fear. In the awesomeness of our belief, may we see you as the God who became human because you love us and from whom we have nothing to fear.

M.B.

The Assumption of the Blessed Virgin Mary
August 15

On this special feast we celebrate that after Mary's death, the risen Jesus took her body and soul to be with him forever in heaven. She shared her life totally with him on earth and through her body he became fully human. Now that her temporary mission on earth was completed, she was assumed by him into heaven, where she was and is the spiritual mother of all his family in his kingdom. Queen of heaven, Mary makes intercession on our behalf with her Son, the King of glory, for all the things we need in this life, so that one day we will enter into our heavenly home.

* * * *

Share the Glory of Your Kingdom

Risen Lord Jesus Christ, we praise you that after her death you took your mother, body and soul, to heaven to share your glory with her. Her assumption was a passing over from this life to a life with you that has no end. On the cross you gave her to us as our mother. We pray that as a risen family we, together with Mary your mother and ours, will someday share in the glory of your heavenly kingdom.

M.B.

May He Do Great Things for Us

Mary, assumed into heaven, be with us in our pilgrimage on earth and encourage us never to lose sight of our eternal destiny. Jesus the Lord has done great things for you. May he through your intercession do great things for us not only in heaven, but in our earthly lives, so that we always witness to his love and power.

M.B.

The Triumph of the Cross
September 14

The cross is the sign of salvation and hope; when Jesus was lifted up on "the tree," he drew everyone to himself. It is by his cross that all our suffering is taken up into the power of his resurrection. He humbled himself even to being condemned to death as a criminal. By his painful death, he showed his love for his Father and for us. We too in all our suffering proclaim that even death has no victory over us as Christians.

* * * *

Love, Courage, and Forgiveness

Lord Jesus, we praise you for love, courage, and forgiveness, which you showed during your agony on the cross. You turned the world of shame into a living tree of love, whose branches reach out to everyone who shelters beneath them. In courage you suffered the brutality of the soldiers and showed yourself as a Prince of peace whose kingdom would not be taken away by violence. You forgave all who had plotted against you, as with your final words you pleaded with your Father on their behalf for forgiveness.

As we gaze upon the cross, may it inspire us to love others without counting the cost. Give us courage to endure in faith all the trials and misunderstandings we suffer and help us to forgive ourselves for any hurt we have inflicted on others.

M.B.

The Symbol of the Cross

Lord Jesus, you died so that we might live the new life of grace. May the cross always be a sign to us that suffering can be creative if it is united with your suffering. May it be for us a symbol of victory not death, of life not despair. May we remember that the cross is not an empty symbol; wherever people suffer injustice and violence you hang on the cross as someone who still suffers with and for people.

M.B.

All Saints
November 1

The saints forever praise God's glory in heaven. In their lives on earth they lived out the Beatitudes preached by Jesus. They modeled their lives on Jesus and often paid the price of martyrdom. We like them should try to live as fully as possible. And with the saints we will eventually share in the happiness and joy of heaven.

* * * *

May We Follow Their Example
Holy Spirit, we have been influenced in our lives by many good people who would be amazed if we told them how much good passed over from their lives into ours. We praise you for our parents and friends who encouraged and taught us about the life of Jesus Christ, not so much by their words as by the example of their lives. You spoke through them; it was evident in their spiritual depth. They made the world a better place. May we in turn follow their example and encourage

those near and dear to us to believe and practice their Christian faith and show their love for Christ in the service of their neighbor.

M.B.

Serving Saints

Lord Jesus, you loved your Father and you showed it by the loving service you gave to everyone during your life on earth. You told us that you came to minister rather than be ministered to; you were a Servant-King who washed your disciples' feet. We live in a human family called the church. May we never assume an attitude of privilege and power in your church, but like you be glad to serve those who need your love and example.

M.B.

All Souls
November 2

As Christians we are a people who put our hope in Christ and his resurrection. Many holy men and women have lived and died before us, and we pray for their eternal happiness with the Lord. Life is an ongoing process through death into unending life. Even though we miss our loved ones, those whose lives we have shared, we are consoled by our belief that we will meet again those whom we have loved and lost awhile.

* * * *

We Pray for Those Who Have Died

Heavenly Father, we thank you that you sent your Son Jesus into our human family so that through his life, death, and resurrection we might hope that we will never be separated even by death from those we love. Life is your most special gift to us, and you will never take it away from us if it is nourished through our faith in your Son. We pray today for our parents and those of our family who have already gone to you, that one day we will be with them again. We pray also for those who need the help of our prayers in their journey home to you, through Jesus Christ our Lord.

M.B.

Forgive Us

Holy Spirit, we commend to your mercy our desire to be forgiven for what we have said or done to cause pain to others who have died. May they be happy in heaven and be filled with the love, peace, and forgiveness that you have promised to those who believe in you.

M.B.

The Immaculate Conception
of the Blessed Virgin Mary
December 8

God the Father chose Mary to be the mother of his Son. From the moment she was conceived in the womb of Anne her mother, Mary was free of sin. This was a unique gift from God, because she was to become the mother of his Son. This was to show his love for her not because of anything she did, but because of what was to happen to her when she said yes to his will for her. We honor her because of God's unique love for her. Through her intercession with God the Father, we pray that Christ be born anew in our lives on this special day of celebration.

* * * *

Pray for Us

Mary Immaculate, star of the morning, may your light shine on our lives and our world as we celebrate the dawn of a new spiritual age in your Son. From the moment of your conception in your mother's womb, God the Father chose you to be the mother of his Son. He decided you would be the vessel of election who would hold this precious treasure in your womb and present it to the world in the Bethlehem stable. Intercede for all families everywhere, that they may know love, harmony, and peace in their homes and grow in favor with God and their fellowman.

M.B.

The Grace to Say Yes

Father, we do not know your plans for us, and yet in all things we pray that we may obey your holy will. Send your Holy Spirit to us that we may be blessed with the gift of discernment and appreciate that what you ask of us is for our spiritual growth and happiness. Give us then the grace to say yes to you, as Mary did at the dawn of salvation.

M.B.

Holy Innocents
December 28

When the three wise men came to worship the infant Jesus in Bethlehem, they were warned not to return to King Herod. Because he was afraid that the baby might become king and threaten his throne, Herod ordered all male children under two years to be slaughtered. On this day we remember all children whose lives were cut short by abortion and ask forgiveness for all their mothers.

* * * *

For Those Who Terminated Their Pregnancies
Lord Jesus, just after your birth, innocent children were killed in Bethlehem because of Herod's fear. I pray for all who have terminated their pregnancies. Assure them that you look after those who have died and are now in your loving care. Help them to live now as peacefully as possible; may they face and confess their actions but in a way that turns them toward your redemption and

forgiveness, not in a way that leads to hopeless guilt and despair. May they forgive themselves as they are forgiven by you. Your forgiveness is the beginning of their new life as they leave behind the shadow of darkness and guilt to walk in a land of light and forgiveness.

M.B.

Lord Jesus, Lover of little children, I pray for all women who have had an abortion. They often carry overpowering guilt and emotional scars. Yet self-recrimination will never bring the baby back. Soothe the minds and hearts of all women who suffer in this way. May they know that their child is happy with you.

M.B.

Part 3

*Special Prayers for People,
Occasions, and Needs*

The Church

God, My Loving Father

Heavenly Father, may the church always teach your love for everyone. I praise and thank you that you knew and loved me even before you formed me in my mother's womb. There is no God like you, and this is why I dare to call you Father. You never stopped loving me even when I did not accept and love myself, because love is of your very nature. You showered me with gifts like the gentle rain from heaven, and I took them all for granted. I forgot you were there and ignored you even though you had branded my name on the palm of your hands. My knowledge of you is so imperfect that as I pray I tend to forget that I am sharing my thoughts with a Father who knows what I need even before the words are on my lips. Be with me this day and all through my life, so that at journey's end I may see you face to face and be happy with you forever.

M.B.

Jesus, My Lord

Jesus, you are my King and Lord of the church you founded on earth. I praise you that you became human and one of us, because you loved us and wanted to share in our life so that we could share in yours. You did not cling to your Godhead but emptied yourself to assume the condition of a servant. By word and action, your love for your Father taught us how precious we are in God's sight. The only prayer you taught us was the Our Father, so that we could identify with you in our attitude to God. No one was so perfect a son as you, because your whole life was Father-oriented. You gave your life completely to everyone you met; you healed people of anything that prevented them from being fully human and alive. You witnessed to God the Father's love for us by giving your life on the cross. You showed us in the church that Christian love costs nothing less than everything. May we gladly pay the price, so that others may know that you are Lord of life in this world and in the world to come.

M.B.

Life in the Holy Spirit

Holy Spirit, you are alive in our church; without you we would not be able to call God our Father or say that Jesus is Lord. You were the Guide of my life, though I was often unaware of your loving, gentle inspiration. In small as well as great events, you were there encouraging me in faith and hope to believe that nothing is impossible to God my Father. You lifted me up when everything seemed meaningless and hollow. You were the Breath beneath my wings as you taught me to fly where eagles dare. You are my Light in darkness, my Hope in despair, my Advocate when I am unforgiving toward myself and others. You are the Source of all that I wish to become, so that my dreams become a reality. From the first day, you hovered over the waters of the universe and will continue to be with us until time is no more. May the love I feel today for God the Father and Jesus my Lord fill me with deep inner peace until you carry me to my longed-for home in heaven.

M.B.

Mary, Mother of the Church

Most holy Mary, you are not only the mother of Jesus, but our mother also. In his agony on the cross Jesus gave you to us, so that in your special way you would be with all Christians, protecting them with your wonderful motherly care.

You are the most unique creation of God our Father, whose will you did when you said yes to his invitation to be the mother of his Son Jesus. Be with all Christians everywhere and intercede for them, so that they may remain true to their Christian calling. May I truly love myself as you would have me, so that I may witness to God's power working in me.

The Holy Spirit overshadowed you when you did not know how the Messiah would be born for us. May the Spirit come to me and fill me with his grace, peace, and love.

I thank you, most blessed Mother, for showing your Son to the world and for sharing him with us. You know how often we fail him because of our human weakness. Teach us to forgive as you forgave those who crucified your Son. May you stand patiently by the foot of my cross as you did that fateful day on Calvary. Pray for me, a sinner, now and at the hour of my death.

M.B.

The Church

God our Father, by the promises you made in the life, death, and resurrection of Christ your Son, you bring together in your Spirit, from all the nations, a people to be your own. Keep the Church faithful to its mission: may it be a leaven in the world renewing us in Christ, and transforming us into your family.

M.B.

The Spread of the Gospel
God our Father, you desire that everyone be saved and come to the knowledge of your truth. Send workers into your great harvest, that the gospel may be preached to every creature, and your people, gathered together by the word of life and strengthened by the power of the sacraments, may advance in the way of salvation and love.

M.B.

Christian Unity
Father, pour out upon us the fullness of your mercy, and by the power of your Spirit remove divisions among Christians. Let your church shine more clearly as a sign for all the nations that the world may be filled with the light of your Spirit and believe in Jesus Christ whom you have sent.

M.B.

Peace
Lord Jesus Christ, you promised your apostles that you would give them your peace. May your followers' faith in this promise preserve that peace in your church to the end of time. May our faith always champion peace as a witness to your abiding presence in the church.

M.B.

For Persecuted Christians

Father, in your mysterious providence, your church must share in the sufferings of Christ your Son. Give us the spirit of compassion and love for those who are persecuted for their faith in you, that they may always be true and faithful witnesses to your promise of eternal life.

M.B.

In Time of Famine

All-powerful Father, God of goodness, you provide for all your creation. Give us in the church an effective love for our brothers and sisters who suffer from lack of food. Help us to do all we can to relieve their hunger, that they may serve you with carefree hearts.

M.B.

For Refugees

Lord, no one is a stranger to you, and no one is ever far from your loving care. In your spirit of caring, may we in the church watch over refugees and exiles, those separated from their loved ones, young people who are lost, and those who have left or run away from home. Bring them back safely to the place where they long to be and help us always to show your kindness to strangers and those in need.

M.B.

For Those Unjustly Deprived of Liberty

Father, your Son came among us as a slave to free the human race from the bondage of sin. May we in the church be in the front lines, trying by every available means to rescue those unjustly deprived of liberty and restore them to the freedom you wish for all your children.

M.B.

Christian Service

Make us worthy, Lord, to serve our fellow men throughout the world who live and die in poverty and hunger. Give them through our hands this day their daily bread, and by our understanding love, give peace and joy.

Mother Teresa

The Homeless

Have mercy, O Lord our God, on those whom war or oppression or famine has robbed of homes and friends, and aid all those who try to help them. We commend also into your care those whose homes are broken by conflict and lack of love; grant that where the love of man has failed, the divine compassion may heal, through Jesus Christ our Lord.

M.B.

In Time of War

God our Father,
Maker and Lover of peace,
to know you is to live,
and to serve you is to reign.
All our faith is in your saving help;
protect us from people of violence
and keep us safe from weapons of hate.
May we in the church always witness to the power of reconciliation rather than that of the sword.

M.B.

For Peace and Justice

God our Father,
you reveal that those who work for peace
will be called your children.
Help us to work without ceasing
for that justice preached and lived
by Jesus your Son,
the justice that brings true and lasting peace.

M.B.

Human Dignity in Employment

Heavenly Father, you have designed our world so that
through our labor we cooperate with you in producing
those goods necessary for life. It is your plan that we should
be engaged in work that enhances rather than hinders our
human dignity. Because of greed and disrespect of the value
of the human person, many are frustrated and unhappy,
their humanity destroyed by the way they are treated as
unimportant components in an uncaring system. Give us
the courage to speak up for the true value of human labor.
May we always be sensitive to the worries and hopes of
those who share with us in our place of employment.

M.B.

God our Father, by our human labor you govern and guide
to perfection the work of creation. Hear the prayers of your
people and give to everyone work that enhances their
human dignity; draw them closer to each other in the service of their brothers and sisters.

M.B.

The Family

For Married Couples

Heavenly Father, you created man and woman, blessed their union, and gave them the earth for their heritage Your Son Jesus looked on this union as something very special and personal. To show his unique respect for husband and wife, he turned water into wine for a young couple at their wedding feast. He saw marriage as essentially a relationship in which the husband and wife grow together by sharing every aspect of their lives. They were not to regard it solely in sexual terms. Send your Spirit into my heart this day, so that I may look on marriage as you did. I pray for all those couples whose love has grown cold. May they rekindle their relationship and realize that marriage is a complete union in which they grow as individuals who have chosen to share their lives together.

M.B.

Preparation for Marriage

Father, we pray for all those contemplating marriage, that they do so with an awareness of their responsibility to make all the emotional and spiritual preparations necessary for such an important decision. May your Spirit help them discern their needs, and may your Son Jesus be with them in a special way on the wedding day.

M.B.

The Family Home

O God, make the door of this house wide enough to receive all who need human love and fellowship and a heavenly Father's care, and narrow enough to shut out all envy, pride, and hate. Make its threshold smooth enough to be no stumbling block to children or to straying feet, but rugged enough to turn back the tempter's power; make it a gateway to your eternal kingdom.

Thomas Ken

Parents, Brothers, and Sisters

Lord Jesus Christ, I praise and thank you for my parents and my brothers and sisters, whom you have given me to cherish. Surround them with your tender, loving care; teach them to love and serve one another in true affection and to look to you in all their needs. I place them all in your care, knowing that your love for them is greater than my own. Keep us close to one another in this life, and lead us at the last to our true and heavenly home.

M.B.

Harmony in the Family

Jesus, you blessed the human family by choosing to spend thirty years in the family home at Nazareth. Bless all families today, so that they may live together in love, peace, and harmony. I pray for all families in which there is damaging discord between siblings. Friendship—understanding the other person—requires time and space in which to grow. Sometimes difficult family dynamics do not give family members the opportunity to discover each other as individuals. I pray to you, Lord, that you enter our homes and fill them again with your peace, as once you did at Nazareth.

M.B.

Gift of Hospitality

Lord Jesus, when you lived in our world, you fed the hungry in the desert and told your apostles that it was their duty to look after those who were hungry. As we thank you for our food and the shelter of our home, give us the mind and heart to welcome the stranger to a place at our table, because in welcoming the stranger we will be welcoming you.

M.B.

Presence of the Holy Spirit

Father, you know that every word we speak, or action we take, has its influence on those we meet; may all we say and do this day be under the influence of the Holy Spirit, so that people may know your power and presence in their lives.

Holy Spirit, fill my mind and heart with love for all my family. May my love for them flow over to those whom they love. Let no word or action of mine ever cause disharmony that would break my family relationships. I thank you for giving me a deep appreciation of my faith and protecting me in situations when it was at risk.

M.B.

For Parents Today

Be with all parents in these days when family values are under attack, and when many children no longer follow their parents' Christian calling. Console and strengthen them so that their pain and disappointment may be lightened by the hope that all will become well in the future, because you watch over and protect them with your unceasing love.

M.B.

Hurt in the Family

Holy Spirit, you hide many things from our knowledge, to spare us anguish and distress. I pray today for all parents and grandparents who are emotionally hurt by their families, especially in moral issues. Give them your grace to sustain them in their time of disappointment and pain. Give them a clearer understanding of the difficulties faced by young people in this modern world that ignores our Christian values. May parents retain a loving relationship with their children, so that when future crises arise, they will be able to assist them gently by example to come to a decision according to your holy will. May they never, however strong the temptation, cut themselves off from the young people of their family but always retain a warm relationship with them, just as our Father does with us, despite our sinfulness and pride.

M.B.

Single People

Father, there are many who feel rejected or abandoned by you, because they have not met the right person with whom to share their lives. As their friends marry, they feel increasingly "left out." I pray for those for whom each day is lonely; their heart-wish to share is not fulfilled. If it be that they never find a partner, grant that their lives will be brightened by and filled with caring friends as a gift from you.

M.B.

Family and Friends

Father, I thank you for all my family and friends. Without them I would feel lonely and unwanted. Sometimes, when I need to be alone with you, the memory of my loved ones, and what they mean to me, warms my heart. They are a gift to me from you, my Father who cares for me at every moment. I pray today for all those who feel lonely, that they too may experience the gift of a loving family of friends. May their lives be enriched by friendship that dispels their loneliness and makes them aware of their value to others and to themselves. Show your love to those who have never really known you, and make them realize that you are their Father from whom all friendship flows.

M.B.

Thank You for Friends

Thank you, Father, for having created us and giving us to each other in the human family. Thank you for being with us in all our joys and sorrows, for your comfort in our sadness, your companionship in our loneliness. Thank you for friends, for health, and for grace.

M.B.

Value of Friendship

Lord Jesus, you sought friends in your life to share your mission and moments of deepest joy and sorrow. Without friendship, inner peace is impossible. The poorest person in the world is the one who has no friends. I am today what people have offered me of themselves in friendship. I pray for all those who are lonely today with no one to share their lives or to notice their comings and goings. Open my heart to them so that with a smile, a gentle touch, an act of kindness, I may lighten their darkness and make them aware that you are smiling and being their Friend through me.

M.B

Expectant Mothers

Father, may the little unborn one who lies close to my heart grow strong day by day until the time of birth. As the delivery draws near, may I not be afraid of the pains but rejoice in the birth of a person destined to share with me in the human family in this world and the world to come.

M.B.

The Gift of a Child

Spirit of Creation, the wonder of life finds its perfect expression in the birth of a child. I thank you for the gift of life. I pray that all parents will look on their children as a blessing from you, and never lose the wonder of how privileged they are to share with you in creation.

M.B.

For the Lonely

Father, in my gratitude to you for giving me family and friends who are very much part of me, I pray for all those who are lonely and feel that no one cares about them. Fill the hearts and minds of lonely people, Father, with sweet memories of those in the past who were kind to them. Send them friends to warm their lives and heal the pain of past memories of loneliness and rejection.

M.B.

Absent Loved Ones

Almighty Father, with love you watch over the affairs of all your children; mercifully hear our prayers for those we love and from whom we are now separated by distance. Be with them, Lord, and protect them in all the trials of life.

Teach us, and them, to feel and know that you are always near, and that we are never parted from each other if we are united in you through Jesus Christ our Lord.

M.B.

For Divorced

Heavenly Father, I pray for all those who are caught up in church law and who because of it are unable to be accepted fully as members of the church community. Be with them in their emotional and spiritual distress and let them know that you have never withdrawn your love from them. Set them free from all thoughts of being misunderstood, abandoned, or rejected as they turn to you for guidance and support, because you alone can lift them up and help them. I thank you that you bring them your healing love to comfort them; let them know that they have our compassionate understanding and our prayers on their behalf.

M.B.

In Times of Difficulty

Trusting God in Difficult Situations

I will trust God.
Whatever I am, I can never be thrown away.
If I am in sickness, my sickness may serve him.

In perplexity, my perplexity may serve him.
He does nothing in vain. He knows what he is about.
He may take away my friends.
He may throw me among strangers.
He may make me feel desolate, make my spirits sink.
Hide my future from me, still he knows what he is about.

John Henry Newman

Healing Prayers Answered

Lord Jesus, when I am faced with difficult situations that neither I nor anyone else can help me to solve, I turn to you as my last and only hope. You never fail me, even though at times the response seems a long time in coming. I thank you that you have answered my prayers for people suffering grave illness. You raised them up, renewed their bodies, and gave them a new spirit of strength and light within them, conquering their weakness and darkness. I thank you, Lord, for the power of your loving healing manifested in so many people who are alive today because you answered their plea for health and healing.

M.B.

Correct Sense of Values

Spirit of Truth, I praise you that you have taught me to value the correct things in life. My love for you is the one constant value that never changes. In all the difficulties I've encountered, I have found you there as my hope and support. Without you, many times I would have failed and not been able to face my problems with courage and conviction. Your love has driven fear out of my life and brought me a sense of belonging and inner security that is my most treasured possession. I pray for all those who feel they cannot cope with life. May they turn to you and discover your love for them, which gives them the strength and understanding to believe in themselves and resolve the problems that cause them anxiety.

M.B.

Correct Attitude to Power

Lord Jesus, Friend of the poor and underprivileged, you gave us the perfect example of what our attitude to rank and power should be. You said if we wanted to be fulfilled, we should seek the kingdom of your Father first, and everything else would fall into place. Power, as the world understands it, was something to be avoided; you told your followers that if they were to be like you, they were not to court secular power, because your kingdom was not of this world. Guide my footsteps, so that I never stray from the true path, because you are my only way to the Father whom I wish to serve in all I say and do.

M.B.

Lifting the Burden

God, my Father, I turn to you in my unrest because I cannot see any way out of the present conflict that troubles my spirit. In my confusion I turn to you for help and guidance, because you alone can help me, and nothing is impossible to you. Light up my life with faith and give me the courage to walk confidently where you lead. You know the right time to lift the burden that oppresses me, and so I place the present moment, as I do my whole life, in your tender care. Put your rest in my mind and your peace in my heart.

M.B.

Value of Suffering

Lord, make me realize that by simply suffering for Jesus' sake, I can often do more for others than by being active in caring for them. It is hard for me to understand this, so please make me accept that my very helplessness in the presence of suffering makes me aware of how much help you have to offer me and those in pain for whom I care. Suffering works mysteriously in a way that is beyond my powers of reasoning, because it creates life and transforms everything it touches when it flows from your cross and from my pain endured for your sake. Open my eyes to see beyond the darkness of suffering to the light and dawn of a new life in the Resurrection.

M.B.

Courage to Carry On

Father, sometimes we feel so oppressed by difficulties on all sides that we want to give up and surrender. At times like these, may we be lifted up in the strong arms of your Son and through him find the courage to continue our struggle, knowing that in your name the victory will eventually be ours.

M.B.

Patience in Praying

Father, it is hard for me, and for so many others, to believe that you listen to our prayers, because at times it seems that our words are falling on deaf ears. Sometimes I have asked and not received, sought and not found, knocked and the door was not opened. At such times, I needed a strong and deep faith to keep persevering in my attempts to have a conversation with you. But when I was tired of talking words to you and sat and listened patiently, you have answered in a wonderful way beyond my hopes and dreams. May I remember those times in the future when I feel tempted to abandon prayer because I think that you are no longer there or you do not care to listen to me. Thank you, Father, for listening.

M.B.

Trusting God My Father

God, you are a loving Father who will not cause us a needless tear. Give me a peaceful heart, at rest in your love for me, and help me to concentrate more on your loving care than on my own preoccupation with physical pain and emotional disturbance.

M.B.

The Positive Aspect of Pain

Father, pain ceases to be barren pain when we believe in faith that you are working through it mysteriously, so that we may grow and be filled with hope like that of a woman giving birth to her child. In all the trials and injustices of life, may we believe that you are in our pain, transforming it through hope into joy, and giving us the strength to overcome all the burdens too difficult for our human frailty to carry alone.

M.B.

In Danger of Losing Our Serenity

Father, you watch over us every moment; be with us this day. When we are tempted to lose our serenity of mind and peace of heart, may your Son Jesus rebuke the inner storms that threaten us. By the power of your Spirit, may we be calm again, knowing that you are always near. Give us the faith to believe in your abiding and never-failing love and protection.

M.B.

Gift of Inner Strength

Father, you do not protect us against suffering, but when we seem to be at the end of our reserves, when darkness seems to engulf us, you give us an inner strength, light, and peace through which we know you have been with us all the time, even in our darkest hours.

M.B.

In Times of Temptation

Lord Jesus, in times of trial and temptation, may I remain close to you, so that I am aware that I do not stand alone. Be my Friend, my Strength, and my Encourager, when I feel I cannot withstand the impulse to indulge my weakness. Teach me not to fear the darkness as long as I look toward you who are my Light and my Hope. In times of darkness and crisis, I have become especially aware of your inspiring light, leading me to believe that with your help I shall overcome. May the experiences I have had of your healing presence encourage me to make others aware of your love and power to help those who in time of temptation call on your holy name.

M.B.

Guilt and Fear

True Sorrow

Lord Jesus, I thank you that you gave your apostles the power to forgive sins in your name and reconcile sinners to your Father, their neighbors, and themselves. Time and again I have told you how sorry I am, yet I still persist in my waywardness. I ask you, Lord, in your goodness, to continue to forgive my failings in the future and set my mind at rest about my past. When you were on earth, you readily forgave sinners and encouraged them to live better lives. I pray that you will do the same for me, so that I experience inner peace because I know that the abundance of your love makes up for my lack of sorrow.

M.B.

Faith That Conquers Fear

Father, take from us all those fears that burden us and bring life to a standstill, making us less human, less free to be ourselves. Give us a faith that conquers fear, so that when fear knocks at our door, we may open it in faith knowing that there is no one there.

M.B.

Awareness of the Father's Love

Father, you loved me even before I was formed in my mother's womb. Your love for me causes me to love myself as a reflection of your never-ending love. Teach me never to fear you; in so doing, I would cloud over your light and condemn myself to live in darkness. Your love for me is my only hope of loving myself and other people. Give me, I pray you, this love that casts out fear, and grant me the true freedom to live as you would have me, a life free from fear and free to love.

M.B.

Trust, the Enemy of Fear

Lord Jesus, let me live this day to the full. Let me fill it with all the wonder and joy I knew as a child. Let me trust and welcome with an open mind and heart all those I meet today, so that this evening I may feel that in some way I have contributed to the joy and peace of the world which you entered so humbly and hopefully, that we might have life to the full.

M.B.

Freedom From Fear

Father, fear is the enemy of my personal freedom and inner peace. Fearful people go through life growing old but never growing up. I am afraid, Father, of being afraid, because it diminishes and destroys my love for you and myself. Send your love into my heart, because only your perfect love can cast out my fear. May I see fear as my enemy, and with your help may I confront all my hidden fears.

M.B.

Healing of Fear

Jesus, our Life and Peace, grant me the grace to believe in your love and mercy. Because you love and understand me, you are merciful in forgiving me all my wrongdoing and weakness. You know that I live in a world damaged by sin, and I need to be protected even from myself. You are my Shepherd and Guide, and with you by my side, I have nothing to fear. My love for you casts out my fear. Teach me to concentrate on your goodness rather than my failings. May I grow more assured that when my life on this earth draws to an end, you will bring me home to your Father to live in love and peace.

M.B.

Guilt From the Past

Father, in the past we may have hurt someone whom we now have no way of contacting. Free us from any guilt we have that prevents us from living our Christian faith to the full as you would have us. Liberate us from the kind of guilt that only helps to foster feelings of self-rejection and hides from us your all-embracing forgiveness. Only you can heal the wounds that have been made and restore everyone to a proper understanding of what true sorrow really means. May all those who live in the shadow of the past walk out into the light of the present, where there is freedom to grow as individuals beloved of you.

M.B.

Being Sorry

Lord Jesus, it is never easy for me to say that I am sorry or to admit that I have been wrong. Saying we are sorry is seen by many as a sign of weakness and of "giving in." You have taught me that although I must be prepared to stand up and be counted in the cause of truth, I should also be humble enough to acknowledge when I am wrong. Put your love of truth in my mind and heart, so that I may always admit my mistakes and never be afraid to say that I am sorry. Bring peace and truth today to all those who are in conflict with another. Teach us all to understand that to say we are sorry requires total honesty, courage, and humility.

M.B.

Freedom From Guilt

Father, in whom there is no past, only the present, teach me always to leave the past behind me, and to live in the present moment, conscious of your loving presence and forgiveness. There have been times in the past when I did not quickly express sorrow for misdeeds that I now regret. Fill me always with an awareness of your mercy as my Father who forgives me, even when I find it difficult to forgive myself. All you ask of me is that I do my best now and praise you for your forgiveness of my past. Make me aware that the dawn of each new day is the beginning of my life in the present and in your presence in which there is no past.

M.B.

Peace With Deceased Family

Father, from whom all fatherhood comes, forgive me for my lack of love for my earthly father who seemed so incapable of loving me like you, my perfect heavenly Father. Help me to remember all the good times I shared with him, so that I may understand him better. He is no longer here for me to talk to. I wish I could have told him I loved him before he died. May I be consoled with the thought that when we meet in heaven, we will both experience love for each other in a new and beautiful way.

M.B.

Healing Hurtful Memories

Heavenly Father, the healing of hurtful memories is a long and delicate process. In them we relive the past, with all its pain renewed in our minds and hearts. Come into the still-painful situations I have experienced and gradually teach me how to forgive as your Son Jesus did. I feel guilty about my lack of forgiveness, though I sense I should admit how deeply hurt I am and that I need your help before I can walk on the road to forgiveness and reconciliation. Remove my feelings of guilt as you peel away the bandages covering my wounds—into which you pour your healing oil of mercy and forgiveness.

M.B.

Worry

Worry Destroys Peace

Lord Jesus, worry is destroying my life. I think of the past with guilt and the future with fear. I worry about everything; it has become so much a part of me that I am unable to feel comfortable in myself unless I have something to worry about. Lord Jesus, you lived in very frightening circumstances, surrounded as you were by prejudice, intrigue, and hypocrisy, yet you never lost your peace. Even on the cross as you were dying, you surrendered the rest of your life to your Father. Put your spirit of peace within me, so that I leave the past to your mercy, put the future in your loving care, and live in the present moment free from worry and full of the joy and challenge of living my life one day at a time.

M.B.

Growing Old

Heavenly Father, I am increasingly aware that I am growing old; the evidence marks my body and slows down my movements. I pray that you will lead me gently through this stage of my life. Increase my awareness of you, so I do not become preoccupied with my increasing mental and bodily fatigue. Deepen my faith and trust in you that all will be well as long as I keep my eyes steadfastly fixed on you. Mellow my memory, so that it dwells only on those things that brought me to a deeper understanding of my loved ones, of you, and of myself. May I live each day to the full, to savor it as wine that has matured with age. And may I share each drop and each moment with you.

M.B.

Entrusting My Life

Lord Jesus, you entrusted your whole life to your heavenly Father. You never worried about the final outcome of any event, even your crucifixion, because you saw worry as a lack of confidence in your Father's willingness and ability to help you. In your many miracles, you called on your Father to witness to his love for you. He never failed to respond. In every situation, may I always seek my Father's kingdom first, knowing that everything I need will be given to me.

M.B.

Father, Be With Me

Worry divides and distracts us from the main thing in life: to give the Father all honor and glory by our trust in him. May I live each day to the full and let tomorrow look after itself, because my Father will be with me tomorrow as surely as he is with me today.

M.B.

Worry Achieves Nothing

Lord Jesus Christ, you told us not to worry or be anxious. You know that each day has enough troubles of its own; we are not to burden ourselves with memories of yesterday's problems or be worried about tomorrow's possible difficulties. Give me then a mind at rest, knowing that my Father is sensitive to all my needs, for which he will provide. Place in my mind the conviction that I do not face any obstacle that may come my way alone, because you are with me to lighten my burden and give strength to my spirit. Tomorrow will look after itself, and yesterday is in your merciful care, because you have already taken it to yourself. So having nothing to fear, I shall with your help live this day, and all the days of my life, in your peace.

M.B.

Inner Peace

Peace the World Cannot Give

Lord Jesus, a peace that the world cannot give is your gift to your followers. Fill my mind and heart with your peace, so that I may look at the world through your eyes and know that your precious gift keeps me serene amid all the trials and tribulations that each day brings. Teach me to discern the peace I should seek, the peace I should keep, and the peace I should share. Peace means loving myself so that I am at peace in every situation. May I see everyone I meet as a possible friend and not a potential enemy. As your peace comes to me like gentle rain or sunshine, so may my peace flow out to others and nourish them, that they, too, may grow through your gift of peace.

M.B.

Peaceful Mind

Father, you do nothing in vain and all things are for our good; give me a mind at peace and a heart at rest, trusting you in all my undertakings, so that, though I may never see the end-result of my labors, I am confident they will come to a successful conclusion through your wisdom, power, and love.

M.B.

Enjoying Life

Lord, eternal Lover of life, help me to savor and enjoy life through every season. May I not waste one moment, always seeing each as your gift to me. Life is an adventure with its challenges and rewards when lived to the full, as your Son Jesus Christ would have me do.

M.B.

Turn My Heart to You

Lord Jesus, turn my heart to you this day. In the depth of my being, with the noise of the world around me stilled and my mind at rest, may I find you present to me as the Giver and Sharer of my peace.

M.B.

Controlling Anger

Lord Jesus Christ, by word and action you have shown us that anger is justifiable on certain occasions. Any anger you expressed was directed at those who abused their position. You saw anger as a necessary emotion, but you controlled your anger and did not let it control you. I ask, Lord, that you give me the gift of using and controlling my anger as you did yours. May I never use it in a way that is a detriment to others or myself. Guide and strengthen me, so that I never shirk my responsibilities in opposing violence and injustice. And when the waves of anger pass, send me your peace to still my spirit, knowing that what I said and did is what you would have done in similar circumstances.

M.B.

Avoiding Jealousy

Lord Jesus, you were the victim of jealousy all through your humble life. The leaders of your own people felt threatened by your mission of love and healing. They were afraid of losing their power as thousands flocked to you, even out into the desert. Secure in your Father's love, you loved people because this is what your Father wanted you to do.

Teach me to be at peace within myself, so that I never lose the awareness of God my Father's love for me. With this I am rich enough and do not ask for anything more. May I learn to be glad at other people's happiness and fulfillment, so that I see it as a blessing for them rather than as a threat to me.

M.B.

Peace in Our World

Holy Spirit, I pray today for peace in our world and an end to violence. May there be peace in our homes and hearts so that we may live and work together in a spirit of peace and harmony. Remind me that I share my world with others, many less fortunate than I am, and maybe resentful. Help me to understand their frustration, which often expresses itself in violence and anger. Purify the minds and attitudes of men and women in leadership, especially in the media, so that they present a better, more peaceful view of our world, rather than the violent image that agitates those troubled in spirit. May the world know Christ's peace, without which society loses its direction and ignores our deep desire for peace.

M.B.

Being a Peacemaker

Father, peace is the great gift of your Son to our world; help us to be peacemakers, so that we build bridges that bring people together and not walls that divide and segregate. In environments of violence and distrust, may we, by our loving understanding, always be part of the solution, never part of the problem.

M.B.

Bringing Peace to Others

Lord Jesus, you came to earth for everyone, so that no one would be excluded from your all-embracing love. Inspire me with the same spirit of generosity, so that I may always remain open, especially to those who have hurt me or toward whom I have nurtured resentment. May this, and every day, be like Christmas, as you inspire me to bring peace and reconciliation to all I meet.

M.B.

Healing

Jesus the Healer

Jesus, our wounded Healer, I believe in you; in all your works, you did the will of your Father and never sought your own glory. You exercised your ministry so that those who witnessed it would give glory to God the Father. You were Father-oriented, and your life was one of prayer. You healed people because you loved them; you never worked miracles in order to be popular. Your humility in acknowledging the source of your power drew people to give thanks to God. Lord Jesus, our Healer, when we pray for healing for others in your name, teach us to act and think as you did, so that people will see you at work in our ministry. May they believe that you are alive and healing people even today.

M.B.

Praying for Healing

Jesus, Healer of the sick, who raised the dead to life, I praise you for the faith you give me to keep on hoping and praying for those who are ill. You know what is best for each person for whom I pray, so I leave the final outcome to your tender mercy.

Listen to the silent tears of those who weep inside their spirits as they yearn to see their loved ones made whole and well again. Your healing of people was the center of your earthly message. In the face of the most severe medical and psychological diagnoses, may we continue to pray for those who are seriously ill, and may your inner peace, which is ultimate healing, come to us all.

M.B.

Depression

Lord, I have known what it is to find myself lost in the valley of darkness and depression. In those times you came to me in fleeting moments with the assurance that all would eventually be well. Today may the power of your Spirit be the breath beneath my wings and bear me up, so that I may fly like an eagle to a place where I shall find light and peace.

M.B.

Healing in the Church Today

Lord Jesus, in every situation you are healing your people from all that injures them. You healed the sick, gave sight to the blind, and even raised the dead to life. When you sent your apostles on their first mission, you told them to cure the sick, raise the dead, cleanse the lepers, and cast out devils. You said you would be with them—your church—always, and this is what you wanted them to do. You are with the church today whenever it heals in your name. I thank you for all the healing of mind, body, and spirit that takes place in your name in every corner of the world. Encourage us to believe in your willingness and power to heal your people. May your healing mission grow as we witness to your name in a world that sorely needs your healing love and presence.

M.B.

Thanksgiving for Healing

Lord Jesus, our Healer, I thank you for your many miracles of healing, not only during your lifetime on earth, but also in our world today. I bless you for your special interventions that have changed people's lives, whether physical, spiritual, or emotional. Through your healing my own life has been changed, even in some ways hidden from me at present. Awaken in me an awareness of all you have done and are doing for me, so that I may proclaim my belief to everyone that you live and heal all those who believe in your name.

M.B.

For Those Who Heal the Sick

Spirit of Healing and Wholeness, I commit all that I am, my body, emotions, and spirit, to your tender care. I thank you for doctors, nurses, and all those who care for the sick. Bless their skills. In trusting them, may I show my total commitment and trust to you. May I never lose this trust, which is the source of my inner peace.

M.B.

Renewal of Faith

Lord Jesus, just as you gave sight to the blind, renew in me my life of faith. Lend me your vision, so that I may see again the beauty of your life and know the thrill of your message, which allows me to see beyond the limits of my own vision. Bless today all who are blind to a personal awareness of you and the healing you bring. Open their eyes, Lord, so that they may see the beauty of your life and world.

M.B.

Sufferers From Asthma

Spirit of God, whose breath fills us with life, breathe today on all those who suffer from asthma. You alone can heal them and bring them peace. Ease the worry of their parents and others who love them, so that any anxiety is not "contagious" throughout the family. May they realize the value of taking life placidly, as your Spirit moves gently into their lives and brings them inner peace.

M.B.

For Spiritual Growth

Lord Jesus, we all need your vision and courage if we are to grow as fulfilled people. You came to a kingdom where people had lost the dream that was part of their heritage. Come again, Jesus, into my life and fill me with your Spirit, so that I may renew the dream you have for me. Rekindle the fire of my enthusiasm for your message, so that it changes me and those I meet. Send a wonderful outpouring of your Spirit on us all, bringing us hope for the future and making our dreams come true.

M.B.

When Suffering Comes

Father, in union with Jesus in Gethsemane, we offer you a heart that trusts you in the dark and a mind at rest in your loving arms, so that when the dawn comes, we may know that you have always been there supporting, strengthening, and healing us.

M.B.

Alcohol and Its Abuse

Lord Jesus Christ, you showed us the value of so many things when used in moderation and on the right occasion. Aware of the terrible consequences to individuals and their families when alcohol is abused, I pray that I shall always use alcohol in such a way that it never controls me.

I pray for all families that have suffered emotionally, physically, and spiritually because of alcoholism. May this abuse in families be brought under control, and any scars be healed.

Increase our understanding of alcoholism and its causes, so that we in the church and the larger world treat its victims with gentleness and firmness.

Lord, through your love for families, protect them from the dangers of alcoholism, and bring peace into their homes.

M.B.

Bereavement

Belief in the Resurrection

Jesus, when you wept over the death of Lazarus, you showed us the value of grieving. You told us that those who grieve would be comforted. I thank you for the gift of tears that helps heal our deep grief in the face of a loved one's death. The tears can represent our sorrow mixed with joy: sorrow that we are physically separated from someone and joy because of our belief that we will meet again, never to part. I thank you for being the Resurrection and the Life. The one who believes in you will never die. The memory of that promise of yours has lightened the burden of sorrow when I grieve.

Comfort all those who as yet have not found solace in their distress. Give them the gift of tears to express their sorrow and also their hope.

M.B.

Comfort in Grieving

Almighty Father, be with all those who grieve today over the loss of a loved one. May their sorrow be lit with the brightness of the Resurrection; may they be assured that they will meet again those whom they have loved and lost awhile. May they know that they are never parted from each other if they are united in Jesus your Son. May he who said that the blessed who mourn shall be comforted, comfort those who grieve today, and strengthen their belief in life after death.

M.B.

Life After Death

Father, your Son Jesus told us that in your house there are many mansions. There is room for us all. This belief in you and your generosity helps me to believe in life after death. I look forward to meeting my parents, brothers, sisters, friends, and all those with whom I shared my life. My belief in the Resurrection is my anchor of hope which keeps the frail boat of my faith secure in the midst of storms and tempest.

M.B.

Seeing Loved Ones Again

My grief is mellowed by the knowledge that death is only a parting for a little while from those whom we love and who love us. May we see our friends and family as a great cloud of witnesses from heaven, surrounding us on all sides, encouraging us to believe that where they are now, we will be one day to share with them in their joy and happiness.

M.B.

Resurrection Peace

Jesus, you have won the victory over Satan. I should be thinking of you and your triumph, rather than concentrating on the power of Satan. I praise you for the example of the people whose belief in your resurrection has brought me a deep peace that nothing or no one can destroy. I know that Satan would like me to think that he has power over me, but my faith in your victory overcomes all his attempts to trap me into thinking of him rather than of you. I pray for all those caught in this snare, so that they may be delivered and become free to acknowledge you as Lord and Savior, in whom there is perfect peace and happiness.

M.B.

Value Life!

Father, Lover of life, you never take back any of your gifts to me. Life is your gift to me, so that even in death I do not lose my life but change it for something more perfect. In my new life I shall see you face to face and know you in a way that is impossible as long as I remain in my mortal body.

Teach me then to value my life now, so that I live each day to the full. Life comes to me moment by moment. Encourage me not to waste a single moment by worrying about the future, especially about what will happen to my loved ones when you come to call me home to you. May I trust them and myself to your tender loving care in which we find our inner peace which nothing can disturb.

M.B.